ultimate
CROCHET
NURSERY

ultimate
CROCHET
NURSERY

40 Designs for Blankets, Baskets, Decor & So Much More

KRISTI SIMPSON

STACKPOLE BOOKS

Guilford, Connecticut
Blue Ridge Summit, Pennsylvania

Published by Stackpole Books
An imprint of Globe Pequot, the trade division of
The Rowman & Littlefield Publishing Group, Inc.
4501 Forbes Blvd., Ste. 200
Lanham, MD 20706
www.rowman.com

Distributed by NATIONAL BOOK NETWORK
800-462-6420

Photography by Heather Alvarado/Heartstrings Photography

We have made every effort to ensure the accuracy and completeness of these instructions. We cannot, however, be responsible for human error, typographical mistakes, or variations in individual work.

British Library Cataloguing in Publication Information available

Library of Congress Cataloging-in-Publication Data

Names: Simpson, Kristi, author.
Title: Ultimate crochet nursery : 40 designs for blankets, baskets, decor & so much more / Kristi Simpson.
Description: Lanham : Stackpole Books, 2022. | Summary: "Kristi Simpson delivers 40 patterns for diverse items for the baby and nursery: blankets, decorative garlands, baskets, car seat cover, pillows, nursing cover-up, lovie and toys, diaper bag, mobile, wipe cozy, pouf, sleepsack, changing mat, wall hangings, rugs, and much more—all in colors and styles for the bright, happy, modern nursery"— Provided by publisher.
Identifiers: LCCN 2021040389 (print) | LCCN 2021040390 (ebook) | ISBN 9780811770002 (paperback) | ISBN 9780811770026 (epub)
Subjects: LCSH: Crocheting—Patterns. | Infants' clothing. | Infants' supplies.
Classification: LCC TT825 .S54633 2022 (print) | LCC TT825 (ebook) | DDC 746.43/4—dc23
LC record available at https://lccn.loc.gov/2021040389
LC ebook record available at https://lccn.loc.gov/2021040390

First Edition

CONTENTS

INTRODUCTION

On the hunt for nursery decorating ideas? Prepping for a new bundle of joy to enter your family is hands down one of the most exciting times in life.

From blankets to toys to rugs and wall art, I've assembled the ultimate collection of crochet items to give that new arrival the most comfortable and functional nursery. After all, that teeny, tiny bundle of joy deserves the best—including some seriously enviable nursery decor.

If you're on a super-tight budget, don't splurge on items before you've crocheted a few of these patterns to customize the nursery just the way you want. There are so many fun options out there that can make even an ordinary object into something exciting and inspiring. Decorate with cute baskets, curtains, sensory cubes, a colorful crib caddy, and make it more sentimental by crocheting it yourself.

To the momma: You'll spend many late nights in this room, so make it cute and comfy. The space that welcomes your baby into the world should boast an inviting, calming, and fun atmosphere full of handmade love. Not to mention, many of these patterns also work as transitional decor and function for years!

To friends and family: The patterns in the book will give the new nursery a handmade, unique, and special feel, as well as being functional. You can't go wrong giving any of these as gifts to the new baby. Some of the items are great for older siblings as well—don't forget them!

This ultimate collection is full of color and inspiration. I hope you find many patterns here that you'll enjoy crocheting for an added touch of yarn-y goodness to your nursery.

Best stitches,
Kristi

Angel Wings Garland

Celebrate the new baby with color! Make a sweet garland in a solid color, or mix it up. Either way, you'll have a sweet handmade banner to decorate the nursery.

Yarn
Knit Picks Dishie; medium weight #4; 100% cotton; 3.5 oz (100 g)/190 yds (174 m) per skein
- 1 skein each: 27040 Ash (**A**), 25404 Creme Brulee (**B**), 25411 Conch (**C**), 27041 Mint (**D**), 25409 Swan (**E**)

Hook and Other Materials
- US size H-8 (5 mm) crochet hook
- Yarn needle

Finished Measurements
Motif: 4 in (10.2 cm) wide x 3½ in (9 cm) long

Gauge
16 sc = 4 in (10.2 cm)
Adjust hook size if necessary to obtain gauge.

Special Stitch
Picot: Ch 3, sl st to first ch.

INSTRUCTIONS

Motif
Make 2 motifs in A, B, D, and E, and 3 motifs in C.
Ch 4, join with sl st to first ch to form ring.
Rnd 1 (RS): Ch 1, sc in ring, (ch 8, sc) 4 times, sl st in ring; join with sl st to first sc. (5 sc, 4 ch-8 sps, 1 sl st)
Rnd 2: Ch 6, 4 sc in next ch-8 sp, (ch 3, 4 sc in next ch-8 sp) 3 times, ch 6, sl st to next sc, ch 4; join with sl st to joining sl st of Rnd 1. (2 ch-6 sps, 16 sc, 3 ch-3 sps, 1 sl st, 1 ch-4 sp)
Rnd 3: Ch 1, (5 sc, ch 3, sc) in ch-6 sp, sc in next 4 sts, 3 sc in ch-3 sp, sc in next 4 sts, (3 sc, picot, 3 sc) in next ch-3 sp, sc in next 4 sts, 3 sc in next ch-3 sp, sc in next 4 sts, (sc, ch 3, 5 sc) in ch-6 sp, 3 sc in next ch-4 sp; join with sl st to first sc. (40 sc, 2 ch-3 sps, 1 picot)
Fasten off.

Fringe
Cut three 6-in (15.2-cm) strands of same color, fold strands in half, pull folded loop end through picot, pull loose ends of folded yarn though center loop, and pull to tighten. Trim evenly.

Joining
With E, ch 30, *sl st to right corner ch-3 with RS facing, ch 12, sl st to left corner ch-3 sp, ch 8; rep from * until all motifs are joined, ending last rep with ch 30.
Fasten off.

Ava Motif Blanket

Make a blanket pop with crochet motif patterns! These aren't your average crochet granny squares, either. This crochet motif blanket pattern adds the perfect touch of fashion and function.

Yarn
Berroco Vintage; worsted weight #4; 52% acrylic/40% wool/8% nylon; 3.5 oz (100 g)/218 yds (199 m) per skein
- 2 skeins each: 5194 Breezeway (**A**), 5176 Pumpkin (**B**)
- 3 skeins: 5108 Stone (**C**)
- 1 skein: 5127 Butternut (**D**)

Hook and Other Materials
- US size J-10 (6 mm) crochet hook
- Stitch marker
- Yarn needle

Finished Measurements
Each motif is approximately 11 in (28 cm)

Gauge
Rnds 1–3 = 6 in (15.2 cm)
14 dc = 4 in (10.2 cm)
Adjust hook size if necessary to obtain gauge.

Special Stitches
Cluster (cl): Yarn over, insert hook in st indicated, yarn over, pull through, yarn over, pull through 2 loops on hook, yarn over, insert hook in same st indicated, yarn over, pull through 2 loops on hook, yarn over, pull through all 3 loops on hook.
Picot: Ch 4, sl st to first ch.
3-Double Crochet Cluster (3-dc cl): Yarn over, insert hook in st indicated, yarn over, pull through, yarn over, pull through 2 loops on hook, (yarn over, insert hook in same st indicated, yarn over, pull through 2 loops on hook) 2 times, yarn over, pull through all 4 loops on hook.

Pattern Notes
- Beginning ch-3 counts as first dc.
- Yarn amount is for 9 motifs and border. If you increase motif counts, increase yarn amount.

INSTRUCTIONS

Motif

With A, ch 5, join.

Rnd 1 (RS): Ch 1, sc in ring, (ch 5, sc in ring) 5 times, ch 5; join with a sl st to first sc. (6 sc, 6 ch-sp)

Rnd 2: Sl st to next ch-sp, ch 3 (counts as first dc), (dc, ch 3, 2 dc) in same sp, ch 2, *(2 dc, ch 3, 2 dc) in next ch-sp, ch 2; rep from * around; join with a sl st to first beg ch-3. [6 (2 dc, ch 3, 2 dc) groups, 6 ch-2 sp] Fasten off.

Rnd 3: Join B in any ch-3 sp, ch 2, dc in same sp, ch 5, cl in next ch-2 sp, ch 5, *cl in next ch-3 sp, ch 5, cl in next ch-2 sp, ch 5; rep from * around; join with sl st to beg ch-3. (12 cl, 12 ch-5 sp)

Rnd 4: Sl st to next ch-5 sp, ch 1, (3 sc, picot, 3 sc) in each ch-sp around; join with a sl st to first sc. (72 sc, 12 picot) Fasten off.

Rnd 5: Join C in any picot loop, ch 1, sl st in same sp, *ch 3, 3-dc cl over Rnd 4 into Rnd 3 cl, ch-3, sl st in next picot; rep from * around; join with a sl st to first sl st. (12 3-dc cl, 24 ch-3 sp, 12 sl st) Fasten off.

Rnd 6: Join D in any ch-3 sp, ch 5 (counts as first dc and ch-2), dc in same sp, (dc, ch 2, dc) in each ch-3 sp around; join with sl st to ch-3 of beg ch-5. [24 (dc, ch 2, dc) groups] Fasten off.

Rnd 7: Join B in any ch-2 sp, ch 3, 3 dc in same sp, 4 dc in next 4 ch-2 sps, (2 tr, ch 2, 2 tr) in next ch-2 sp, *4 dc in next 5 ch-2 sps, (2 tr, ch 2, 2 tr) in next ch-2 sp; rep from * around; join with sl st to beg ch-3. [80 dc, 4 (2 tr, ch 2, 2 tr) groups] Fasten off.

Rnd 8: Join A in ch-2 sp in corner, ch 3, 4 dc in same sp, *(hdc in next, ch 1, sk 1) 12 times**, 5 dc in next ch-2 sp; rep from * around, ending last rep at **; join with sl st to beg ch-3. (48 hdc, 48 ch-1 sp, 20 dc) Fasten off.

Rnd 9: Join C in 3rd dc in any corner, ch 3, 2 dc in same st, ch 1, *dc in next 28 sts and ch-1 sps across, ch 1**, 3 dc in next st, ch 1; rep from * around, ending last repeat at **; join with sl st to beg ch-3. (112 dc, 8 ch-1 sp, 4 3-dc corners)

Rnd 10: Sl sl to next st, ch 1, *3 sc in corner, hdc in next st, hdc in ch-1 sp, hdc in next 8 sts, sc in next 12 sts, hdc in next 8 sts, hdc in ch-1 sp, hdc in next st; rep from * around; join with sl st to first sc. (140 sts) Fasten off.

Joining

Block each square before joining (optional).
Use whipstitch or other method of choice to join squares.

Edging

Rnd 1: With RS facing, join C in 2nd dc in any corner, ch 3, 2 dc in same st, *dc in each st across to second sc in corner**, 3 dc in corner; rep from * around, ending last rep at **; join with sl st to beg ch-3. (106 sts) Fasten off.

Rnd 2: Join A in second dc in any corner, ch 1, (cl, ch 1, cl) in same st, ch 1, sk 1 st, *cl in next st, ch 1, sk 1 st ** rep from * across to next corner, (cl, ch 1, cl) in second dc in corner; rep from * around, ending last rep at **; join with sl st to first cl. [53 cl per side (212 total), 54 ch-1 sp per side (216 ch-1 sp total), 4 (cl, ch 1, cl) groups in corners] Fasten off.

Rnd 3: Join B in ch-1 sp in any corner, (ch 3, picot, dc, picot, dc) in same sp, *[(dc, picot, dc) in next ch-1 sp, sk next cl] across to ch-1 sp in next corner**, (dc, picot, dc, picot, dc) in corner; rep from * across, ending last rep at **; join with sl st to first corner. [54 (dc, picot, dc) groups per side (216 total), 4 (dc, picot, dc, picot, dc) groups in corners] Fasten off.

Finishing
Weave in ends.

Monster Pillow

Can't you hear funny roars mixed with silly stories? Playtime has never been more fun than with a monster pillow!

Yarn

Lion Brand Vanna's Choice; worsted weight #4; 100% acrylic; 3.5 oz (100 g)/170 yds (156 m) per skein
- 2 skeins 860-110 Navy (**A**)
- 1 skein each: 860-153 Black (**B**), 860-100 White (**C**)

Lion Brand Yarns Fun Fur; bulky weight #5; 100% polyester; 1.75 oz (50 g)/64 yds (58 m) per skein
- 2 skeins: 320-350A Deep Sea (**D**)

Hook and Other Materials
- US size H-8 (5 mm) crochet hook
- Yarn needle
- Poly-Fil stuffing
- Stitch markers

Finished Measurements
17½ in (44.5 cm) tall

Gauge
12 sc and 12 rows = 4 in (10.2 cm) with A and D held together
Adjust hook size if necessary to obtain gauge.

Special Stitch
Single Crochet 2 Together (sc2tog): (Insert hook, yarn over, pull up loop) in each of the stitches indicated, yarn over, draw through all loops on hook. See photo tutorial on page 167.

Pattern Notes
- Beg ch-3 counts as first dc.
- Beg ch-2 will not count as a stitch.
- The front will be 5 rows shorter than the back due to the extra thickness from working with 2 yarns held together in the first section.
- Use stitch markers to hold 2 panels together evenly when sewing together.

INSTRUCTIONS

Back
Row 1 (RS): With A, ch 21, 2 sc in second ch from hook, sc in next 18 sts, 2 sc in last st. (22 sc)
Row 2: Ch 1, turn, 2 sc in first st, sc in next 20 sts, 2 sc in last st. (24 sc)
Row 3: Ch 1, turn, 2 sc in first st, sc in next 22 sts, 2 sc in last st. (26 sc)
Row 4: Ch 1, turn, sc in each st across.
Row 5: Ch 1, turn, 2 sc in first st, sc in next 24 sts, 2 sc in last st. (28 sc)
Row 6: Ch 1, turn, 2 sc in first st, sc in next 26 sts, 2 sc in last st. (30 sc)
Row 7: Ch 1, turn, sc in each st across.
Row 8: Ch 1, turn, 2 sc in first st, sc in next 28 sts, 2 sc in last st. (32 sc)
Row 9: Ch 1, turn, 2 sc in first st, sc in next 30 sts, 2 sc in last st. (34 sc)
Rows 10–48: Ch 1, turn, sc in each st across. Do not fasten off.

Horn 1
Row 1: Continuing with A, ch 1, sc in next 10 sts, leave remaining sts unworked. (10 sc)
Row 2: Turn, sc2tog, sc in next 8 sts. (9 sc)
Row 3: Ch 1, turn, sc in each st across.
Row 4: Turn, ch 1, sc2tog, sc in next 7 sts. (8 sc)
Row 5: Ch 1, turn, sc in each st across.
Row 6: Ch 1, turn, sc2tog, sc in next 4 sts, sc2tog. (6 sc)
Row 7: Ch 1, turn, sc in each st across.
Row 8: Ch 1, turn, sc2tog, sc in next 2 sts, sc2tog. (4 sc)
Row 9: Turn, ch 1, (sc2tog) 2 times. (2 sc)
Fasten off.

Horn 2
Turn back panel, and join A in last stitch of Row 48. Rep Rows 1–9 of Horn 1.

Front
Row 1 (RS): With A and D held together, ch 21, 2 sc in second ch from hook, sc in next 18 sts, 2 sc in last st. (22 sc)
Row 2: Ch 1, turn, 2 sc in first st, sc in next 20 sts, 2 sc in last st. (24 sc)
Row 3: Ch 1, turn, 2 sc in first st, sc in next 22 sts, 2 sc in last st. (26 sc)
Row 4: Ch 1, turn, sc in each st across.
Row 5: Ch 1, turn, 2 sc in first st, sc in next 24 sts, 2 sc in last st. (28 sc)
Row 6: Ch 1, turn, 2 sc in first st, sc in next 26 sts, 2 sc in last st. (30 sc)
Row 7: Ch 1, turn, sc in each st across.
Row 8: Ch 1, turn, 2 sc in first st, sc in next 28 sts, 2 sc in last st. (32 sc)
Row 9: Ch 1, turn, 2 sc in first st, sc in next 30 sts, 2 sc in last st. (34 sc)
Rows 10–37: Ch 1, turn, sc in each st across. Fasten off D.
Rows 38–43: With A, ch 1, turn, sc in each st across. Do not fasten off.

Horns
Repeat Horn 1 and 2 for Front.

Trim (Front and Back)
Join A in any stitch, work sc evenly around panel, using stitches and ends of row as stitches; join with sl st to first sc.
Fasten off.

Eye (make 2)
Rnd 1 (RS): With C, ch 4, 7 dc in 4th ch from hook; join with a sl st to first dc. (8 dc)
Rnd 2: Ch 2, 2 dc in each st around; join with a sl st to first dc. (16 dc)
Rnd 3: Ch 2, *dc in next st, 2 dc in next st; rep from * around; join with sl st to first dc. (24 dc)
Rnd 4: Ch 2, *dc in next 2 sts, 2 dc in next st; rep from * around; join with sl st to first dc. (32 dc)
Rnd 5: Ch 1, *sc in next 3 dc, 2 sc in next dc; rep from * around; join with sl st to first sc. (40 sc)
Fasten off, leaving a long tail for sewing.

Pupil (make 2)
Rnd 1 (RS): With B, ch 4, 9 dc in 4th ch from hook; join with sl st to first dc. (10 dc)
Fasten off, leaving a long tail for sewing.

Mouth
Rnd 1 (RS): Using B, ch 4, 10 dc in 4th ch from hook; join with sl st to first dc. (10 dc)
Rnd 2: Ch 2, 2 dc in each st around; join with sl st to first dc. (20 dc)
Rnd 3: Ch 2, *dc in next st, 2 dc in next dc; rep from * around; join with sl st to first dc. (30 dc)
Fasten off, leaving a long tail for sewing.

Teeth (make 2)
Row 1 (RS): Using C, ch 2, sc in 2nd ch from hook. (1 sc)
Row 2: Ch 1, turn, 2 sc in first st. (2 sc)
Row 3: Ch 1, turn, sc in each st across.
Row 4: Ch 1, turn, 2 sc in each st. (4 sc)
Fasten off, leaving a long tail for sewing.

Assembly
Using photos as guide for placement:
Sew pupil to eye.
Sew teeth to mouth.
Sew eyes and mouth to front.
With WS together, use stitch markers to hold panels in place. Working through both panels, with A, sl st panels together, stuffing pillow firmly before closing.

Baby Catchall Tote

In a hurry? Have this catchall tote ready for those quick trips to town. It's large enough to hold all of the basic necessities without needing to have the main bag in tow.

Yarn
Patons Lincoln Fog; medium weight #5; 75% acrylic/25% wool; 3.5 oz (100 g)/190 yds (174 m) per skein
- 1 skein each: Bark (**A**), Wisteria (**B**), Mother of Pearl (**C**)

Hook and Other Materials
- US size I-9 (5.5 mm) crochet hook
- 1 belt cut into two 20-in (50.8-cm) straps
- Nail and hammer (to add sewing holes to straps)
- Sewing thread and needle
- Yarn needle

Finished Measurements
Base: 14 in (35.5 cm) wide x 4¼ in (11 cm) deep
Bag: 11 in (28 cm) high

Gauge
12 sc and 12 rows = 4 in (10.2 cm)
Adjust hook size if necessary to obtain gauge.

Special Stitches
Reverse Single Crochet (rev sc): Single crochet worked from left to right (right to left, if left-handed). Insert hook into next stitch to the right (left), under loop on hook, and draw up a loop. Yarn over, draw through all loops on hook. See photo tutorial on page 173.
Single Crochet 2 Together (sc2tog): (Insert hook, yarn over, pull up loop) in each of the stitches indicated, yarn over, draw through all loops on hook. See photo tutorial on page 167.

Pattern Notes
- When changing colors, fasten off yarn each round for a clean finish.
- The beg ch-2 does not count as st.
- The beg ch-4 will count as first dc and ch-1.
- For photo tutorials on working into the back loop (BLO) and working around stitch posts, see pages 162 and 170.

INSTRUCTIONS

Base
Row 1 (WS): With A, ch 13, sc in 2nd ch from hook and in each ch across. (12 sc)
Rows 2–42: Ch 1, turn, sc in each st across. Do not turn on last row.

Body
Begin working in rounds.
Rnd 1 (RS): Ch 1, [sc 42 evenly across ends of rows, sc in next 12 sts] twice, join. (108 sc)
Rnd 2: Ch 1, working in BLO, sc in each st around; join with sl st to first sc.
Rnds 3–9: Ch 1, sc in each st around; join with a sl st in first sc. Drop A; join B.
Rnd 10: With B, ch 2 (not a st here or throughout), dc in each st around; join with sl st to first dc.
Rnd 11: Ch 2, *dc in next 2 sts, dc around last 2 posts just made, sk next unworked st; rep from * around; join with sl st to first dc. Drop B; join C.
Rnd 12: Rep Rnd 10.
Rnd 13: With C, sl st to next st, ch 4 (counts as dc and ch-1), sk 2 sts, (dc, ch 1, dc) in next st, *sk 2 sts, (ch 1, dc, ch 1) in next st, sk 2 sts, (dc, ch 1, dc) in next st; rep from * around to last 2 sts, ch 1, sk 2 sts; join with sl st to ch-3 of beg ch-4.
Rnd 14: Ch 2, dc in each st around; join with sl st to first dc.

Rnd 15: Ch 4, dc in same st, ch 1, sk 2 sts, dc in next st, ch 1, sk 2 sts, *(dc, ch 1, dc) in next st, sk 2 sts, (ch 1, dc, ch 1) in next st, sk 2 sts; rep from * around; join with sl st to ch-3 of beg ch-4. Fasten off C; join B.
Rnds 16–18: Rep Rnds 10–12. Fasten off B; join A.
Rnd 19: With A, ch 1, sc in each st; join with sl st to first sc. (108 sc)
Rnd 20: Ch 1, *sc in next 7 sts, sc2tog; rep from * around; join with sl st to first sc. (96 sc)
Rnds 21–22: Ch 1, sc in each st around; join with sl st to first sc.
Rnd 23: Ch 1, *sc in next 10 sts, sc2tog; rep from * around; join with sl st to first sc. (88 sc)
Rnds 24–25: Ch 1, sc in each st around, and join with sl st to first sc.
Rnd 26: Ch 1, rev sc in each st around; join with sl st to first sc.
Fasten off.
Weave in ends.

Assembly
Use hammer and nail to add 4 holes in ends of each strap.
Use sewing needle and thread to stitch handles in place.

Stuffed Rattle Toy

Give your child the sweetest and quietest rattle! Enjoy crocheting a fun stuffed toy that the baby can safely play with!

Yarn

Knit Picks Swish Worsted; medium weight #4; 100% superwash merino wool; 1.75 oz (50 g)/110 yds (100 m) per skein

- 1 skein each: 26068 Conch (**A**), 24662 White (**B**), 26066 Honey (**C**)

Hook and Other Materials

- US size C-2 (2.75 mm) crochet hook
- Yarn needle
- Poly-Fil stuffing

Finished Measurements

6 in (15.2 cm) long

Gauge

5 sc x 5 rows = 1 in (2.5 cm)
Adjust hook size if necessary to obtain gauge.

Special Stitch

Single Crochet 2 Together (sc2tog): (Insert hook, yarn over, pull up loop) in each of the stitches indicated, yarn over, draw through all loops on hook. See photo tutorial on page 167.

Pattern Notes

- The rattle is made from the base to the top of rattle.
- When changing colors, complete the stitch until the last pull-through; drop working yarn, pull through next color as last pull-through to complete color change, and finish stitch. See photo tutorial on page 174.

INSTRUCTIONS

With A, ch 2.

Rnd 1 (RS): 4 sc in 2nd ch from hook; join with sl st to first sc. (4 sts)

Rnd 2: Ch 1, 2 sc in each st around; join with sl st to first sc. (8 sts)

Rnd 3: Ch 1, *sc in next st, 2 sc in next st; rep from * around; join with sl st to first sc. (12 sts)

Rnds 4–5: Ch 1, sc in each st around; join with sl st to first sc.

Rnd 6: Ch 1, *sc in next st, sc2tog; rep from * around; join with sl st to first sc. (8 sts) Fasten off A; join B.

Stuff firmly as you go.

Rnd 7: Ch 1, sc in each st around; join with sl st to first sc. Fasten off B; join C.

Rnds 8–9: Ch 1, sc in each st around; join with sl st to first sc. Fasten off C; join B.

Rnds 10–21: Rep Rnds 7–9.

Rnd 22: Ch 1, 2 sc in each st around; join with sl st to first sc. (16 sts)

Rnd 23: Ch 1, *sc in next st, 2 sc in next st; rep from * around; join with sl st to first sc. (24 sts)

Rnd 24: Ch 1, *sc in next 2 sts, 2 sc in next st; rep from * around; join with sl st to first sc. (32 sts)

Rnd 25: Ch 1, *sc in next 3 sts, 2 sc in next st; rep from * around; join with sl st to first sc. (40 sts)

Rnds 26–28: Ch 1, sc in each st around; join with sl st to first sc. Fasten off B; join A.

Rnd 29: Ch 1, sc in each st around; join with sl st to first sc. Fasten off A; join B.

Rnd 30: Ch 1, sc in each st around; join with sl st to first sc. Do not fasten off B.

Rnd 31: Ch 1, work sc in B, change to A (see Pattern Notes), *sc in next st, change to B, sc in next st, change to A; rep from * around; join with sl st to first sc. Fasten off A; join B.

Rnd 32: Ch 1, sc in each st around; join with sl st to first sc. Fasten off B; join A.

Rnd 33: Ch 1, sc in each st around; join with sl st to first sc. Fasten off A; join B.

Rnds 34–35: Ch 1, sc in each st around; join with sl st to first sc.

Rnd 36: Ch 1, *sc in next 3 sts, sc2tog; rep from * around; join with sl st to first sc. (32 sts)

Rnd 37: Ch 1, *sc in next 2 sts, sc2tog; rep from * around; join with sl st to first sc. (24 sts)

Stuff firmly.

Rnd 38: Ch 1, *sc in next st, sc2tog; rep from * around; join with sl st to first sc. (16 sts)

Rnd 39: Ch 1, (sc2tog) 8 times; join with sl st to first sc. (8 sts)

Rnd 40: Ch 1, sc in each st around; join with sl st to first sc.

Fasten off, leaving a long tail for sewing.

Finishing

Thread yarn needle with long end and close top.
Weave in ends.

Snuggle Time
Sleepersack

As newborns, our twins had to be tightly swaddled or else they would not sleep. And as parents, we know how valuable our sleep is with new babies!

Yarn

Knit Picks Wool of the Andes; medium weight #4; 100% Peruvian Highland wool; 1.8 oz (50 g)/110 yds (100 m) per skein
- 2 skeins: 25975 Creme Brulee

Hook and Other Materials
- US size J-10 (6 mm) crochet hook
- Yarn needle

Finished Measurements

10.5 in (26.7 cm) wide x 14 in (35.5 cm) long

Gauge

8 dc x 4 rows = 2 in (5 cm)
Adjust hook size if necessary to obtain gauge.

Special Stitches

Beginning Cluster (Beg cl): Ch 2, *yarn over, insert hook in st or sp indicated, yarn over and pull up a loop, yarn over and draw through 2 loops on hook; rep from * one more time, yarn over and draw through all 3 loops on hook.

Cluster (cl): *Yarn over, insert hook in st or sp indicated, yarn over and pull up a loop, yarn over and draw through 2 loops on hook; rep from * 2 times more, yarn over and draw through all 4 loops on hook.

Front Post Double Crochet (FPdc): Yarn over, insert hook from front to back around post of st indicated, yarn over and pull up a loop (3 loops on hook), (yarn over and draw through 2 loops on hook) twice. See photo tutorial on page 170.

Back Post Double Crochet (BPdc): Yarn over, insert hook from back to front around post of st indicated, yarn over and pull up a loop (3 loops on hook), (yarn over and draw through 2 loops on hook) twice. See photo tutorial on page 171.

Pattern Notes
- The sleepersack is made from the bottom to the top.
- Do not leave baby unattended while sleepersack is in use.

INSTRUCTIONS

Ch 4.

Rnd 1 (RS): 12 dc in first ch; join with sl st to first dc. (12 sts)

Rnd 2: Ch 2 (not a st here and throughout), 2 dc in each st; join with sl st to first dc. (24 sts)

Rnd 3: Ch 2, *dc in next st, 2 dc in next st; rep from * around; join with sl st to first dc. (36 sts)

Rnd 4: Ch 2, *dc in next 2 sts, 2 dc in next st; rep from * around; join with sl st to first dc. (48 sts)

Rnd 5: Ch 2, *dc in next 3 sts, 2 dc in next st; rep from * around; join with sl st to first dc. (60 sts)

Rnd 6: Ch 2, *dc in next 9 sts, 2 dc in next st; rep from * around; join with sl st to first dc. (66 sts)

Rnd 7: (Beg cl, ch 1, cl) in first st, sk 2 sts, *(cl, ch 1, cl) in next st, sk 2 sts; rep from * around; join with sl st to Beg cl.

Rnd 8: Ch 3, dc in each ch sp and cl around; join with sl st to beginning ch-3.

Rnds 9–24: Rep Rnds 7 and 8.

Rnds 25–26: Ch 2, *FPdc on next st, BPdc on next st; rep from * around; join with sl st to first FPdc.

Fasten off. Weave in ends.

Trendy Diaper Pail Cover

A plain diaper pail doesn't add much to your room decor, so let's spice it up! With a pretty yarn and fun design, that pail might still be stinky, but it will be pretty!

Yarn
Berroco Pixel; light weight #3; 100% superwash wool; 3.5 oz (100 g)/328 yds (300 m) per skein
- 3 skeins: 2251 Mojito

Hook and Other Materials
- US size 7 (4.5 mm) crochet hook
- Yarn needle

Finished Measurements
About 18 in (45.7 cm) wide x 30 in (76.2 cm) long (see Pattern Notes for instructions to adjust size to fit your pail)

Gauge
14 sc = 4 in (10.2 cm)
Adjust hook size if necessary to obtain gauge.

Special Stitch
3-Double Crochet Cluster (3-dc cl): Yarn over, insert hook in st indicated, yarn over, pull through st, yarn over, pull through 2 loops on hook, (yarn over, insert hook in same st, yarn over, pull through st, yarn over, pull through 2 loops on hook) 2 times, yarn over, pull through all 4 loops on hook.

Pattern Notes
- The beginning ch-3 counts as first dc.
- Adjust width by beginning with any even chain number.
- Adjust length by measuring and repeating Rows 2–5 until length is reached.

INSTRUCTIONS
Ch 100.

Row 1 (RS): Sc in 2nd ch from hook and in next ch, *ch 1, sk 1 ch, sc in next ch; rep from * across to last 3 chs, ch 1, sk 1 ch and sc in last 2 chs. (51 sc, 48 ch-1 sps)

Row 2: Ch 4 (counts as dc and ch-1), turn, *sk next sc, 3-dc cl in next ch-1 sp, ch 1; rep from * across to last ch-1 sp, 3-dc cl in last ch-1 sp, ch 1, sk next sc, dc in last sc. (2 dc, 48 3-dc cl, 48 ch-1 sps)

Row 3: Ch 1, turn, sc in first st, sc in next ch-1 sp, *ch 1, sk next 3-dc cl, sc in next ch-1 sp; rep from * across to last ch-1 sp, sc in last ch-1, sc in last st. (51 sc, 48 ch-1 sps)

Row 4: Ch 1, turn, sc in first st, ch 1, sk next st, *sc in next ch-1 sp, ch 1, sk 1; rep from * across, ending with sc in last st. (50 sc, 49 ch-1 sps)

Row 5: Rep Row 3.

Rows 6–149: Rep Rows 2–5 thirty-six times or to desired length.

Trim
Ch 1, do not turn. Working down edge, sc evenly in ends of each row to end, 3 sc in corner (about 151), sc in each st of foundation chain, 3 sc in corner (about 101 sc), working up edge, sc evenly in each row to end, 3 sc in corner (about 151 sc), sc in each stitch across, 3 sc in last corner, sl st to first sc (about 101 sc). (about 504 sc total)

Fasten off. Weave in ends.

Finishing
Cut three 12-in (30.5-cm) lengths of yarn. Tie at top, bottom, and middle of Row 1.

Wrap cover around diaper pail, tie through opposite side of cover.

Precious
Hanging
lanterns

Perk up any corner in the nursery with these fun and whimsical lanterns. Mix and match colors to coordinate and keep the baby entertained!

Yarn

Lion Brand Truboo; light weight #3; 100% rayon; 3.5 oz (100 g)/241 yds (220 m) per skein
- 1 skein each: 837-100 White (**A**), 837-156 Mint (**B**)

Hook and Other Materials

- US size G-6 (4 mm) crochet hook
- 6 in (15.2 cm) diameter steel ring (3 mm thick)
- Yarn needle

Finished Measurements

About 8 in (20 cm) long, 6 in (15.2 cm) diameter

Gauge

About 20 dc = 4 in (10.2 cm)
Adjust hook size if necessary to obtain gauge.

Pattern Note

The beginning ch-3 counts as first dc.

INSTRUCTIONS

Make 1 in A and 1 in B.

Rnd 1 (RS): Working over the steel ring, join with a ch 5 (counts as first dc and ch 2), (dc, ch 2) 31 more times on ring; join with sl st to ch-3 of beg ch-5. (32 dc, 32 ch-2 sps)

Rnd 2: Sl st to next ch-2 sp, ch 5 (counts as first dc and ch-2), sk 1 dc, *(dc, ch 2) in next ch-1 sp, sk 1 dc; rep from * around; join with sl st to ch-3 of beg ch-5. (32 dc, 32 ch-2 sps)

Rnd 3: Ch 3, 2 dc in next ch-2 sp, *dc in next dc, 2 dc in next ch-2 sp; rep from * around; join with sl st to beg ch-3. (96 dc)

Rnd 4: Ch 3, dc in next 2 sts, ch 5, sk 5 sts, *dc in next 3 sts, ch 5, sk 5 sts; rep from * around; join with sl st to beg ch-3. (36 dc, 12 ch-5 sps)

Rnd 5: Sl st in next 2 dc, sl st to next ch-5 sp, ch 3, 8 dc in same sp, sk 3 dc, *9 dc in next ch-5 sp, sk 3 dc; rep from * around; join with sl st to beg ch-3. (96 dc)

Hanging

Cut two 20-in (50.8-cm) strands. Hold these strands together and overhand knot the middle together to create a hanging loop. You will have four strands to attach to the hoop. At this point, the easiest way to work is to suspend the hanging loop from a hook. You could also slip the small loop over the top of a hanger, and then hang the hanger from a doorknob. Wrap strand over and around hoop every 8 sps, drawing out the strand so that the large ring hangs 9 in (23 cm).

Rnd 6: Sl st in next 3 dc, ch 3, dc in next 2 sts, ch 5, sk 6 sts, *dc in next 3 sts, ch 5, sk next 6 sts; rep from * around; join with sl st to beg ch-3.

Rnds 7–13: Rep Rnds 5 and 6 until piece measures 7 in (18 cm), ending on Rnd 5.

Fasten off. Weave in ends.

Briar Wall Hanging

Add color and style to your wall with this stunning wall hanging. It's made in simple rows using bold color and texture.

Yarn
Universal Deluxe Bulky Superwash; bulky weight #5; 100% superwash; 3.5 oz (100 g)/106 yds (97 m) per skein
• 4 skeins: 903 Terra Cotta

Hook and Other Materials
• US size J-10 (6 mm) crochet hook
• Yarn needle
• 18-in (46-cm) dowel rod

Finished Measurements
Approximately 21 in (53 cm) wide and 21 in (53 cm) long, excluding fringe

Gauge
12 sts x 13 rows = 4 in (10.2 cm)
Adjust hook size if necessary to obtain gauge.

Special Stitch
Popcorn Stitch (pc): Work 4 dc in same st, drop loop from hook, insert hook from front to back in top of first dc made, pick up dropped loop and draw through loop on hook: pc made.

INSTRUCTIONS
Ch 62.
Row 1 (RS): Sc in second ch from hook and in each ch across. (61 sc)
Row 2: Ch 1, turn, sc in first 3 sc, *ch 3, sk 2 sc, pc in next sc, ch 3, sk 2 sc, sc in next 5 sc, rep from * across, ending last rep with sc in last 3. (6 pc, 31 sc, 12 ch-3 sps)
Row 3: Ch 1, turn, sc in first 3 sc, *3 sc in ch-3 sp, sc in pc, 3 sc in ch-3 sp, sc in next 5 sc; rep from * across, ending last rep with sc in last 3 sts. (73 sc)

Row 4: Ch 6 (counts as dc and ch 3), turn, sk first 4 sc, *sc in next 5 sc**, ch 3, sk 3 sc, pc in next sc, ch 3, sk 3 sc; rep from * across, ending last rep at **, ch 3, dc in last sc.

Row 5: Ch 1, turn, sc in first dc, 3 sc in ch-3 sp, *sc in next 5 sc, 3 sc in ch-3 sp, sc in pc, 3 sc in ch-3 sp; rep from * across, ending last rep with 3 sc in turning ch-lp, sc in 3rd ch of turning ch-lp. (73 sc)

Row 6: Ch 1, turn, sc in first 3 sc, *ch 3, sk 3 sc, pc in next sc, ch 3, sk 3 sc, sc in next 5 sc; rep from * across, ending last rep with sc in last 3 sc.

Rows 7–54: Rep Rows 3–6 twelve more times or until desired length.

Fasten off. Weave in ends.

Fringe

Cut thirty-eight 15-in (38-cm) strands of yarn. Fold two strands of yarn together in half. With crochet hook, draw fold through edge of wall hanging, forming a loop. Pull yarn through this loop and pull to tighten.

Continue attaching fringes evenly along folded edge of wall hanging.

Trim fringe ends evenly.

Assembly

Use yarn needle and a long length of yarn to sew through top stitches of hanging to dowel rod.

Hanging

Cut a 30-in (76.2-cm) length of yarn. Create a slip-knot on each end of strand and slip over each end of dowel rod. Adjust length by adjusting one end of strand.

Blooming Wall Hanging

Add a burst of color to your nursery! This beautiful mandala wall hanging will be the perfect addition to the baby decor!

Yarn
Willow Yarns Meadow; medium weight #4; 100% cotton; 1.75 oz (50 g)/103 yds (95 m) per skein
- 1 skein each: 0016 Phlox (**A**), 0005 Goldenrod (**B**), 0037 Gooseberry (**C**), 0008 Leaf (**D**)

Hook and Other Materials
- US size H-8 (5 mm) crochet hook
- Yarn needle
- 10 in (25.5 cm) diameter hoop

Finished Measurements
10 in (25.5 cm) diameter

Gauge
14 sc x 16 rows = 4 in (10.2 cm)
Adjust hook size if necessary to obtain gauge.

Special Stitches
3-Double Crochet Cluster (3-dc cl): Yarn over, insert hook in st indicated, yarn over, pull through st, yarn over, pull through 2 loops on hook, (yarn over, insert hook in same st, yarn over, pull through st, yarn over, pull through 2 loops on hook) 2 times, yarn over, pull through all loops on hook.

3-Treble Crochet Cluster (3-tr cl): Yarn over twice, insert hook in st, yarn over, pull through st, (yarn over, pull through 2 loops on hook) twice, [yarn over twice, insert hook in same st, yarn over, pull through st, (yarn over, pull through 2 loops on hook) twice] 2 times, yarn over, pull through all loops on hook.

Pattern Notes
- When changing colors, complete the stitch before the color change until the last pull-through; drop working yarn, pull through next color as last pull-through to complete color change, and finish stitch. See photo tutorial on page 174.
- The beginning ch-3 counts as first dc.
- The beginning ch-4 counts as first dc plus ch 1.

INSTRUCTIONS

With A, ch 6; join with sl st to first ch to form a ring.

Rnd 1 (RS): Ch 3 (counts as dc), 9 dc in ring; join with sl st to beg ch-3. (10 dc) Fasten off A.

Rnd 2: Join B, ch 4 (counts as first dc and ch-1), (dc, ch 1) in each st around; join with sl st to ch-3 of beg ch-4. (10 dc, 10 ch-1 sps) Fasten off.

Rnd 3: Join C in any ch-1 sp, ch 3, 2 dc in same st, ch 1, sk 1 dc, *3 dc in next ch-1 sp, ch 1, sk 1 st; rep from * around; join with sl st to beg ch-3. (30 dc, 10 ch-1 sp) Fasten off C.

Rnd 4: Join D, sl st in next ch-1 sp, ch 3, 2 dc in same sp, ch 3, sk 3 dc, *3 dc in next ch-1 sp, ch 3, sk 3 dc; rep from * around; join with sl st to beg ch-3. (30 dc, 10 ch-3 sp) Fasten off.

Rnd 5: Join A in 2nd dc of any 3-dc set, ch 1, sc in same st, sk 1 dc, *(ch 2, 3 dc-cl, ch 3, 3-tr cl, ch 3, 3-dc cl, ch 2) in next ch-3 sp, sk 1 dc**, sc in next dc; rep from * around, ending last rep at **; join with sl st to first sc. (10 sc, 10 cl sets) Fasten off.

Rnd 6: Join B in top of 3-tr cl, ch 1, sc in same st, ch 8, *sc in next 3-tr cl, ch 8; rep from * around; join with sl st to first sc. (10 sc, 10 ch-8 sps) Fasten off.

Rnd 7: Join C in any ch-8 sp, ch 3, (3 dc, ch 3, 4 dc) in same sp, ch 4, sk next sc, *(4 dc, ch 3, 4 dc) in next ch-8 sp, ch 4, sk next sc; rep from * around; join with sl st to beg ch-3. [10 (4 dc, ch 3, 4 dc) sets, 10, ch-4 sps] Fasten off.

Rnd 8: Working over hoop, join D in any ch-3 sp, ch 3, (3 dc, ch 3, 4 dc) in same sp, ch 3, sk 4 dc, sc in ch-4 sp, ch 3, sk 4 dc, *(4 dc, ch 3, 4 dc) in next ch-3 sp, ch 3, sk 4 dc, sc in next ch-4 sp, sk 4 dc; rep from * around; join with sl st to beg ch-3. [10 (4 dc, ch 3, 4 dc) groups, 20 ch-3 sps, 10 sc] Fasten off.

Weave in ends.

Diamond Curtains

Shade your sweet baby with handmade curtains. With a simple diamond design and a li'l flair of color, these curtains will definitely soften up the baby's room.

Yarn
Berroco Modern Cotton DK; light weight #3; 60% pima cotton/40% modal rayon; 3.5 oz (100 g)/335 yds (306 m) per skein
- 2 skeins each: 6600 Bluffs (**A**), 6660 Coast (**B**), 6603 Piper (**C**), 6618 Coffee Milk (**D**)

Hook and Other Materials
- US size G-6 (4 mm) crochet hook
- Yarn needle

Finished Measurements
About 31 in (78 cm) long x 29 in (73.5 cm) wide

Gauge
14 sc x 16 rows = 4 in (10.2 cm)
Adjust hook size if necessary to obtain gauge.

Pattern Notes
- When changing colors, complete the stitch before the color change until the last pull-through; drop working yarn, pull through next color as last pull-through to complete color change, and finish stitch. See photo tutorial on page 174.
- The beginning ch-4 counts as first dc plus ch 1.
- The curtain is made in horizontal stripes. If you want to alter the curtain length, use the count of 16 + 2 for horizontal. Depending on hanging preference, you'll alter width if you hang horizontal and length if you hang vertical. The curtains shown in photos are hung with vertical stripes.

INSTRUCTIONS

Panel (make 2)

With A, ch 162.

Row 1 (RS): Dc in 6th ch from hook (counts as dc, ch 1, and sk 1 sp), *ch 1, sk 1, dc in next ch; rep from * across. (80 dc, 79 ch-1 sps)

Rows 2–4: Ch 4 (counts as dc and ch-1 here and throughout), turn, sk 1 st, dc in next dc, *ch 1, sk 1, dc in next dc; rep from * across. (80 dc, 79 ch-1 sps)

Row 5: Ch 4, turn, sk next ch-1 sp, dc in next dc, (ch 1, sk next ch, dc in next st) 6 times, dc in next ch-1 sp, dc in next dc, *(ch 1, sk next ch, dc in next ch) 7 times, dc in next ch-1 sp, dc in next st; rep from * across to last 14 sts, (ch 1, sk next ch, dc in next ch) 7 times. (89 dc, 70 ch-1 sps)

Row 6: Ch 4, turn, sk next ch-1 sp, dc in next dc, *(ch 1, sk next ch, dc in next st) 5 times, dc in each of next 6 sts; rep from * across to last 12 sts, (ch 1, sk next ch-1 sp, dc in next dc) 6 times, ending with ch 1 and dc in last st. (107 dc, 52 ch-1 sps)

Row 7: Ch 4, turn, sk next ch-1 sp, dc in next st, (ch 1, sk next ch, dc in next st) 4 times, *dc in next 4 sts, ch 1, sk next st, dc in next 5 sts, (ch 1, sk next ch, dc in next st) 3 times; rep from * across to last 4 sts, (ch 1, sk next ch-1 sp, dc in next dc) twice, ending with dc in last st. (116 dc, 43 ch-1 sps)

Row 8: Ch 4, turn, sk next ch-1 sp, dc in next dc, (ch 1, sk next ch-1 sp, dc in next st) 3 times, *dc in next 4 sts, (ch 1, sk next ch-1 sp, dc in next dc) 3 times, dc in next 4 sts, ch 1, sk next ch-1 sp, dc in next dc; rep from * across to last 8 sts, (ch 1, sk next ch-1 sp, dc in next st) 3 times, ending with dc in last st. (116 dc, 43 ch-1 sps)

Row 9: Ch 4, turn, sk next ch-1 sp, dc in next dc, (ch 1, sk next ch-1 sp, dc in next st) twice, *dc in next 4 sts, (ch 1, sk next ch-1 sp, dc in next st) 5 times, dc in next 2 sts; rep from * across to last 8 sts, dc in next 2 sts, (ch 1, sk next ch-1 sp, dc in next dc) 3 times, ending with dc in last st. (108 dc, 51 ch-1 sps)

Row 10: Rep Row 8.

Row 11: Rep Row 7.

Row 12: Rep Row 6.

Row 13: Ch 4, turn, sk next ch-1 sp, dc in next st, (ch 1, sk next ch-1 sp, dc in next st) 6 times, *dc in next 2 sts, (ch 1, sk next ch-1 sp, dc in next st) 6 times, *dc in next 2 sts, (ch 1, sk next ch-1 sp, dc in next st) 7 times; rep from * across, ending with ch 1 and dc in last st. (89 dc, 70 ch-1 sps)

Row 14: Ch 4, turn, sk next ch-1 sp, dc in next st, (Ch 1, sk next ch-1 sp, dc in next st) 6 times, ch 1, sk 1 dc, dc in next dc), * (ch 1, sk next ch-1 sp, dc in next dc) 7 times, ch 1, sk 1 dc, dc in next dc; rep from * across to last 14 chs, (ch 1, sk next ch-1 sp, dc in next st) 7 times. (80 dc, 79 ch-1 sps)

Rows 15–16: Ch 4 (counts dc and ch-1 here and throughout), turn, sk 1 st, dc in next dc, *ch 1, sk 1, dc in next dc; rep from * across. (80 dc, 79 ch-1 sps) Fasten off.

Change to B.

Rows 17–61: Rep Rows 2–16 changing to color C, D at ends of Row 16. End with Row 13.

Row 62: Rep Row 16.

Fasten off. Weave in ends.

Kolby Mandala Rug

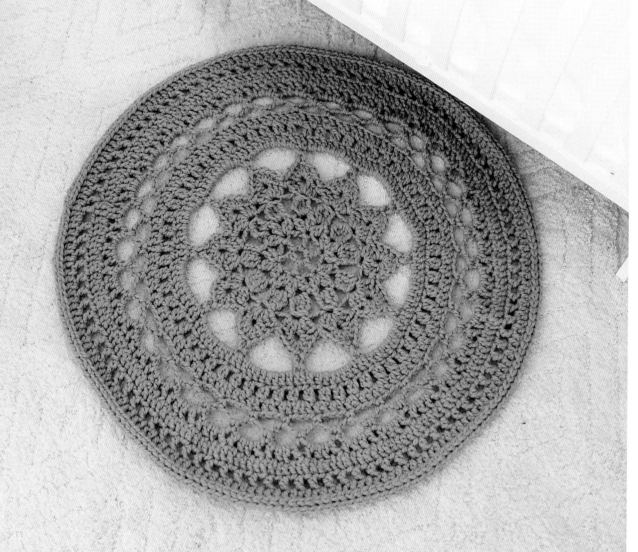

Don't forget your floors! Add a soft and chunky rug and a bit of whimsy with this mandala-style rug. This will not only look cute but also keep your feet warm on those late nights!

Yarn

Lion Brand Wool Ease Thick and Quick; super bulky weight #6; 80% acrylic/20% wool; 12 oz (340 g)/212 yds (194 m) per skein
- 2 skeins: 641-102 Clay

Hook and Other Materials
- US size M/N-13 (9 mm) crochet hook
- Yarn needle

Finished Measurements

Approximately 34 in (86.4 cm) in diameter

Gauge

8 dc = 4 in (10.2 cm)
Adjust hook size if necessary to obtain gauge.

Special Stitches

Beginning 2-Double Crochet Cluster (Beg cl): Ch 2, yarn over, insert hook in same st, yarn over and pull up loop, yarn over and draw through first 2 loops, yarn over and pull through all loops on hook.

2-Double Crochet Cluster (cl): (Yarn over, insert hook in st, yarn over and pull up loop, yarn over and draw through first 2 loops) twice, yarn over and pull through all loops on hook.

3-Treble Crochet Cluster (3-tr cl): Yarn over twice, insert hook in st, yarn over and pull up a loop, (yarn over and draw through first 2 loops) twice, [yarn over twice, insert hook in same st, yarn over and pull up loop, (yarn over and draw through first 2 loops) twice] twice, yarn over and pull through all loops on hook.

4-Treble Crochet Cluster (4-tr cl): Yarn over twice, insert hook in stitch, yarn over and pull up loop, (yarn over and draw through first 2 loops) twice, [yarn over twice, insert hook in same st, yarn over and pull up loop, (yarn over and draw through first 2 loops) twice] 3 times, yarn over and pull through all loops on hook.

Picot: Ch 3, sl st to first ch.

Back Post Single Crochet (BPsc): Insert hook from back to front to back around post of st indicated, yarn over and pull up a loop, yarn over and draw through 2 loops on hook. See photo tutorial on working into stitch posts on page 170.

Pattern Notes
- Beg ch-3 counts as first dc unless otherwise instructed.
- Beg ch-4 counts as first dc and ch 1.

INSTRUCTIONS
Ch 5; join with sl st to first ch to form a ring.

Rnd 1 (RS): Ch 7 (counts as tr and ch 1), *tr, ch 3 in ring 5 times; join with sl st to ch-4 of beg ch-7. (6 tr, 6 ch-3 sps)

Rnd 2: Beg cl, (ch 3, cl, ch 3, cl) in same sp, (cl, ch 3, cl, ch 3, cl) in each tr around; join with sl st to beg cl. (18 cl, 12 ch-3 sps)

Rnd 3: Sl st to next ch-3 sp, ch 4, 3-tr cl in same sp, ch 3, (4-tr cl, ch 3) in each ch-3 sp around; join with sl st to first cl. (12 cl, 12 ch-3 sps)

Rnd 4: Ch 3, (2 dc, ch 2, 3 dc) in same st, sk next ch-3 sp, *(3 dc, ch 2, 3 dc) in next cl, sk next ch-3 sp; rep from * around; join with sl st to beg ch-3. [12 (3 dc, ch 2, 3 dc) groups]

Rnd 5: Sl st to next ch-2 sp, ch 3, (dc 3, picot, dc 3) in same sp, ch 1, sk next 3 dc, sc in space between last skipped dc and next dc, ch 1, sk 3 dc, *4 dc, picot, 3 dc in next ch-2 sp, ch 1, sk 3 dc, sc in space between last skipped dc and next dc, ch 1, sk 3 dc; rep from * around. [12 (4 dc, picot, 3 dc) groups, 24 ch-1 sps, 12 sc]

Rnd 6: Sl st to next picot, ch 1, sc in picot loop, ch 8, *sc in next picot, ch 8; rep from * around; join with sl st to first sc. (12 sc, 12 ch-8 sps)

Rnd 7: Ch 3, dc in same st, 8 dc in ch-3 sp, *2 dc in next sc, 8 dc in ch-3 sp; rep from * around; join with sl st to beg ch-3. (120 dc)

Rnd 8: Beg cl, ch 1, sk 1 st, *cl in next st, ch 1, sk 1 st; rep from * around; join with sl st to beg cl. (60 cl, 60 ch-1 sps)

Rnd 9: Sl st to next ch-1 sp, ch 3, 2 dc in same sp, (sk 1 cl, 2 dc in next ch-1 sp) 4 times, *sk 1 cl, 3 dc in next sp, (sk 1 cl, 2 dc in next ch-1 sp) 4 times; rep from * around, ending with sk 1 cl; join with sl st to beg ch-3. (132 dc)

Rnd 10: Ch 1, sc in same st, ch 5, sk 3 sts, *sc in next st, ch 5, sk 3 sts; rep from * around to last 3 sts, ending with ch-2, dc in first sc. (33 sc, 33 ch-5 sps, 1 ch-2, 1 dc)

Rnd 11: Ch 1, sc in same ch-sp, *ch 6, sc in next ch-sp; rep from * around to last ch-sp, ch 2, dc in first sc. (33 sc, 33 ch-6 sps, 1 ch-2, 1 dc)

Rnd 12: Ch 4 (first dc and ch 1), dc in same sp, (dc, ch 1, dc) 2 times in each ch-6 sp around, ending with (dc, ch 1, dc) in first ch-sp; join with sl st to beg ch-3. [66 (dc, ch 1, dc) groups]

Rnd 13: Ch 3, dc in each st and ch-1 sp around; join with sl st to beg ch-3. (198 dc)

Rnd 14: Ch 4, sk 1 st, *dc in next st, ch 1, sk 1 st; rep from * around; join with sl st to ch-3 of beg ch-4. (99 dc, 99 ch-1 sps)

Rnd 15: Ch 3, dc in each st and ch-1 sp around; join with sl st to beg ch-3. (198 sts)

Rnd 16: Ch 1, BPsc around each st; join with sl st to first st.

Fasten off. Weave in ends.

Baby Butterfly

This butterfly will make a wonderful gift for the new baby (and big sister too). Grab your most colorful yarns, and try this pattern right away!

Yarn
Willow Yarns Meadow; medium weight #4; 100% cotton; 1.75 oz (50 g)/103 yds (95 m) per skein
- 1 skein each: 0013 Thistle (**A**), 0002 Cream (**B**), 0037 Gooseberry (**C**), 0019 Pebble (**D**)

Hook and Other Materials
- US size D-3 (3.25 mm) crochet hook
- Yarn needle
- Two 10-mm safety eyes
- Poly-Fil stuffing
- Stitch markers

Finished Measurements
Approximately 6½ in (16.5 cm) high

Gauge
10 sc = 2 in (5 cm)
Adjust hook size if necessary to obtain gauge.

Special Stitch
Single Crochet 2 Together (sc2tog): (Insert hook, yarn over, pull up loop) in each of the stitches indicated, yarn over, draw through all loops on hook. See photo tutorial on page 167.

Pattern Note
When changing colors, complete the stitch before the color change until the last pull-through; drop working yarn, pull through next color as last pull-through to complete color change, and finish stitch. See photo tutorial on page 174.

INSTRUCTIONS

Body
Rnd 1 (RS): With A, create magic ring, 4 sc in ring; do not join. (4 sc) Place marker to indicate beginning of rnd.
Note: Loop a short piece of yarn around any stitch to mark Rnd 1 as RS. Stuff as you make each section of body. Move stitch marker up with each rnd.
Rnd 2: 2 sc in each sc around. (8 sc)

Rnd 3: *Sc in next st, 2 sc in next st; rep from *
around. (12 sc)

Rnd 4: Sc in each st around.

Rnd 5: (Sc2tog) 6 times. (6 sc)

Rnd 6: 2 sc in each st around. (12 sc)

Rnd 7: *Sc in next st, 2 sc in next st; rep from *
around. (18 sc)

Rnds 8–10: Sc in each st around.

Rnd 11: *Sc in next st, sc2tog; rep from * around.
(12 sc)

Rnd 12: (Sc2tog) 6 times. (6 sc)

Rnd 13: 2 sc in each st around. (12 sc)

Rnd 14: *Sc in next st, 2 sc in next st; rep from *
around. (18 sc)

Rnd 15: *Sc in next 2 sts, 2 sc in next st; rep from *
around. (24 sc)

Rnds 16–18: Sc in each st around.

Rnd 19: *Sc in next 2 sts, sc2tog; rep from *
around. (18 sc)

Rnd 20: *Sc in next st, sc2tog; rep from * around.
(12 sc)

Join B, fasten off A.

Rnd 21: 2 sc in each st around. (24 sc)

Rnd 22: *Sc in next 3 sts, 2 sc in next st; rep from *
around. (30 sc)

Rnds 23–30: Sc in each st around.

Rnd 31: *Sc in next 3 sts, sc2tog; rep from *
around. (24 sc)

Add safety eyes between Rnd 27 and Rnd 28 about
3 sts apart.

Rnd 32: *Sc in next 2 sts, sc2tog; rep from *
around. (18 sc)

Stuff firmly.

Rnd 33: *Sc in next st, sc2tog; rep from * around.
(12 sc)

Rnd 34: (Sc2tog) 6 times. (6 sc)

Fasten off, leaving a long tail for sewing.

Thread yarn needle with long tail and sew top
closed.

Cap

Rnd 1 (RS): With C, create magic ring, 6 sc in ring;
do not join. (6 sc) Place marker to indicate beginning of rnd.

Note: Loop a short piece of yarn around any stitch
to mark Rnd 1 as right side. Move stitch marker
up with each rnd.

Rnd 2: 2 sc in each sc around. (12 sc)

Rnd 3: *Sc in next st, 2 sc in next st; rep from *
around. (18 sc)

Rnd 4: *Sc in next 2 sts, 2 sc in next st; rep from *
around. (24 sc)

Rnds 5–12: Sc in each st around.

To finish, sl st to first sc of last round.

Fasten off, leaving a long tail for sewing.

Thread yarn needle with long tail and sew to head.

Antenna

Join D in post stitch of hat where antenna will be,
ch 4. Fasten off and pull last loop tight.

Rep about 5–6 sts apart.

Flower

With B, ch 2.

Rnd 1 (RS): 5 sc in 2nd ch from hook. (5 sc)

Rnd 2: (Sl st, ch 1, dc, ch 1, sl st) in each st around;
join with a sl st to first st of Rnd 1.

Fasten off, leaving a long tail for sewing.

Thread yarn needle with long tail and sew to cap.

Top Wing (make 4)

Rnd 1 (RS): With D, create magic ring, 11 dc in
ring; join with sl st to first dc. (11 dc) Join C, fasten off D.

Rnd 2: Ch 1, sc in first st, sc in next st, 2 sc in next
st, sc in next st, 2 dc in next st, 3 dc in next st,
2 dc in next st, sc in next st, 2 sc in next st, sc in
next 2 sts; join with sl st to first sc. (17 sts) Join
B, fasten off C.

Rnd 3: Ch 1, sc in first st, sc in next sc, 2 sc in next st, sc in next st, hdc in next st, 2 dc in next st, dc in next st, 2 dc in next st, 3 tr in next st, 2 dc in next st, dc in next st, 2 dc in next st, hdc in next st, sc in next st, 2 sc in next st, sc in next 2 sts; join with sl st to first sc. (25 sts) Join D, fasten off B.

Rnd 4: Ch 1, sc in first st, sc in next 4 sts, 2 hdc in next st, hdc in next 3 sts, dc in next 2 sts, 2 dc in next st, (dc, tr, dc) in next st, 2 dc in next st, dc in next 2 sts, hdc in next 3 sts, 2 hdc in next st, sc in next 5 sts; join with sl st to first sc. (31 sts) Fasten off.

Assembly

Place WS of 2 top wings together, thread D through yarn needle and sew both wings together. Rep with remaining 2 wings.

Bottom Wing (make 4)

Rnd 1 (RS): With C, create magic ring, 11 dc in ring; join with sl st to first dc. (11 dc)

Rnd 2: Ch 1, sc in first st, sc in next st, 2 sc in next st, sc in next st, 2 dc in next st, 3 dc in next st, 2 dc in next st, sc in next st, 2 sc in next st, sc in next 2 sts; join with sl st to first sc. (17 sts) Join D, fasten off C.

Rnd 3: Ch 1, sc in first st, sc in next sc, 2 sc in next st, sc in next st, hdc in next st, 2 dc in next st, dc in next st, 2 dc in next st, 3 tr in next st, 2 dc in next st, dc in next st, 2 dc in next st, hdc in next st, sc in next st, 2 sc in next st, sc in next 2 sts; join with sl st to first sc. (25 sts) Fasten off.

Assembly

Place WS of 2 bottom wings together, thread D through yarn needle and sew both wings together. Rep with remaining 2 wings.

Finishing

Sew points of each set of wings together securely.

Sew joined wings to back of body.

Cut a 4-in (10.2-cm) length of D. Tie a knot at joining of body and head and tie a bow. Trim evenly.

Thread D in yarn needle and stitch on a mouth on the head.

Timmy the Turtle

The cuteness of this little turtle is so heart-melting! Mix it up with girly shades of pink and violet, or have fun with orange and yellows! Not only a toy but cute decor too!

Yarn

Willow Yarns Meadow; worsted weight #4; 100% cotton; 1.75 oz (50 g)/103 yd (95 m) per skein
- 1 skein each: 0032 Pines (**A**), 0006 Succulent (**B**)

Hook and Other Materials

- US size D-3 (3.25 mm) crochet hook
- Yarn needle
- Poly-Fil stuffing
- Black thread or embroidery floss
- Sewing needle
- Stitch markers

Finished Measurements

5 in (12.5 cm) long

Gauge

16 sc x 20 rows = 4 in (10.2 cm)
Adjust hook size if necessary to obtain gauge.

Special Stitches

Single Crochet 2 Together (sc2tog): (Insert hook, yarn over, pull up loop) in each of the stitches indicated, yarn over, draw through all loops on hook. See photo tutorial on page 167.

Back Post Single Crochet (BPsc): Insert hook from back to front to back around post of st indicated, yarn over and pull up a loop, yarn over and draw through 2 loops on hook. See photo tutorial on working into stitch posts on page 170.

Pattern Notes

- When changing colors, complete the stitch before the color change until the last pull-through; drop working yarn, pull through next color as last pull-through to complete color change, and finish stitch. See photo tutorial on page 174.

- Turtle is made in 6 pieces: 1 shell/body, 1 head, 2 arms, and 2 legs.

INSTRUCTIONS

Shell/Body
With A, create a magic ring.
Rnd 1 (RS): 6 sc in ring; do not join. (6 sc)
Note: Do not join; work in continuous rnds (spiral). Place a marker in last st made to indicate end of rnd. Move marker up as each rnd is completed.
Rnd 2: 2 sc in each st around. (12 sc)
Rnd 3: *Sc in next st, 2 sc in next st; rep from * around. (18 sc)
Rnd 4: *Sc in next 2 sts, 2 sc in next st; rep from * around. (24 sc)
Rnd 5: *Sc in next 3 sts, 2 sc in next st; rep from * around. (30 sc)
Rnd 6: *Sc in next 4 sts, 2 sc in next st; rep from * around. (36 sc)
Rnds 7–12: Sc in each st around.
Fasten off.

Rnd 13: Join B, ch 1, BPsc in each st around.
Rnd 14: Working in the round, sc in each st around.
Rnd 15: *Sc in next 4 sts, sc2tog; rep from * around. (30 sc)
Rnd 16: *Sc in next 3 sts, sc2tog; rep from * around. (24 sc)
Rnd 17: *Sc in next 2 sts, sc2tog; rep from * around. (18 sc)
Rnd 18: *Sc in next st, sc2tog; rep from * around. (12 sc) Stuff firmly.
Rnd 19: (Sc2tog) 6 times. (6 sc)
Fasten off, leaving a long tail for sewing. Sew opening closed.

Front Legs (make 2)
With B, create a magic ring.
Rnd 1 (RS): 6 sc in ring; do not join. (6 sc)
Note: Do not join; work in continuous rnds (spiral). Place a marker in last st made to indicate end of rnd. Move marker up as each rnd is completed.
Rnd 2: 2 sc in each st around. (12 sc)

Rnd 3: *Sc in next st, 2 sc in next st; rep from * around. (18 sc)
Rnd 4: *Sc in next 2 sts, 2 sc in next st; rep from * around. (24 sc)
Rnd 5: *Sc in next 3 sts, 2 sc in next st; rep from * around. (30 sc)
Rnd 6: *Sc in next 4 sts, 2 sc in next st; rep from * around. (36 sc) Do not stuff.
Fasten off. Fold in half, sew edges together.

Back Legs (make 2)
With B, create a magic ring.
Rnd 1 (RS): 6 sc in ring; do not join. (6 sc)
Note: Do not join; work in continuous rnds (spiral). Place a marker in last st made to indicate end of rnd. Move marker up as each rnd is completed.
Rnd 2: 2 sc in each st around. (12 sc)
Rnd 3: *Sc in next st, 2 sc in next st; rep from * around. (18 sc)
Rnd 4: *Sc in next 2 sts, 2 sc in next st; rep from * around. (24 sc)
Rnd 5: *Sc in next 3 sts, 2 sc in next st; rep from * around. (30 sc) Do not stuff.
Fasten off. Fold in half, sew edges together.

Head
With B, create a magic ring.
Rnd 1 (RS): 6 sc in magic ring; do not join. (6 sc)
Rnd 2: 2 sc in each st. (12 sc)
Rnd 3: *Sc in next st, 2 sc in next st; rep from * around. (18 sc)
Rnd 4: *Sc in next 2 sts, 2 sc in next st; rep from * around. (24 sc)
Rnd 5: *Sc in next 3 sts, 2 sc in next st; rep from * around. (30 sc)
Rnds 6–10: Sc in each st around.
Rnd 11: *Sc in next 3 sts, sc2tog; rep from * around. (24 sc)
Rnd 12: *Sc in next 2 sts, sc2tog; rep from * around. (18 sc)
Rnd 13: *Sc in next st, sc2tog; rep from * around. (12 sc)
Stuff firmly.
Rnd 14: *Sc in next st, sc2tog; rep from * around. (8 sc)
Rnds 15–17: Sc in each st around. Do not stuff neck.
Fasten off, leaving a long tail for sewing.

Finishing
Sew front and back legs on body.
Sew neck onto body on Rnd 13, where the shell meets the body.
Sew head to shell to help support and tilt upward.
With black thread or embroidery floss, use photo as a guide and stitch on eyes.
Weave in ends.

Cloud Car Seat Hanging Toy

My grandmother would sing "You are my sunshine, my only sunshine" to me as I was growing up, and that has never left me. I think of her often as I see the rays of sunshine coming through those dark cloudy days. Crochet your own little rainbow raindrop cloud toy to brighten the day.

Yarn

Lion Brand Feels Like Butta; medium weight #4; 100% polyester; 3.5 oz (100 g)/218 yds (199 m) per skein
- 1 skein each: 215-100 White (**A**), 215-108 Dusty Blue (**B**), 215-157 Yellow (**C**), 215-156 Mint (**D**)

Hook and Other Materials
- US size G-6 (4 mm) crochet hook
- Yarn needle
- Poly-Fil Stuffing
- 2 Velcro sticky dots

Finished Measurements

8 in (20 cm) wide x 4 in (10.2 cm) high

Gauge

16 sc = 4 in (10.2 cm)
Adjust hook size if necessary to obtain gauge.

Special Stitches

Single Crochet 2 Together (sc2tog): (Insert hook, yarn over, pull up loop) in each of the next 2 stitches indicated, yarn over, draw through all loops on hook. See photo tutorial on page 167.
Single Crochet 3 Together (sc3tog): (Insert hook, yarn over, pull up loop) in each of the next 3 stitches indicated, yarn over, draw through all loops on hook.

Pattern Notes
- When changing colors, complete the stitch before the color change until the last pull-through; drop working yarn, pull through next color as last pull-through to complete color change, and finish stitch. See photo tutorial on page 174.
- Beginning ch-2 of a round will not count as a stitch unless otherwise indicated.
- The beginning ch-3 counts as first dc.

INSTRUCTIONS

Cloud (make 2)

With A, ch 4.
Row 1 (RS): 2 sc in 2nd ch from hook, sc in next 2 chs. (4 sc)
Row 2: Ch 1, turn, sc in next 3 sts, 2 sc in next st. (5 sc)
Row 3: Ch 1, turn, 2 sc in first st, sc in next 4 sts. (6 sc)
Rows 4–5: Ch 1, turn, sc in each st across.
Row 6: Ch 1, turn, sc in next 4 sts, 2 sc in next 2 sts. (8 sc)
Row 7: Ch 1, turn, 2 sc in first 2 sts, sc in next 6 sts. (10 sc)
Row 8: Ch 1, turn, sc in next 9 sts, 2 sc in next st. (11 sc)
Row 9: Ch 1, turn, 2 sc in first st, sc in next 10 sts. (12 sc)
Row 10: Ch 1, turn, sc in next 11 sts, 2 sc in next st. (13 sc)
Rows 11–12: Ch 1, turn, sc in each st across.
Row 13: Ch 1, turn, sc3tog, sc in next 10 sts. (11 sc)
Row 14: Ch 1, turn, sc in next 9 sts, sc2tog. (10 sc)
Row 15: Ch 1, turn, 2 sc in next 2 sts, sc in next 8 sts. (12 sc)
Row 16: Ch 1, turn, sc in next 11 sts, 2 sc in next st. (13 sc)
Row 17: Ch 1, turn, 2 sc in next 2 sts, sc in next 11 sts. (15 sc)
Row 18: Ch 1, turn, sc in next 14 sts, 2 sc in next st. (16 sc)
Rows 19–22: Ch 1, turn, sc in each st across.
Row 23: Ch 1, turn, sc2tog, sc in next 14 sts. (15 sc)
Row 24: Ch 1, turn, sc in next 12 sts, sc3tog. (13 sc)
Row 25: Ch 1, turn, sc3tog, sc in next 10 sts. (11 sc)
Row 26: Ch 1, turn, sc in next 9 sts, sc2tog. (10 sc)
Row 27: Ch 1, turn, sc2tog, sc in next 8 sts. (9 sc)
Row 28: Ch 1, turn, sc in next 6 sts, sc3tog. (7 sc)
Row 29: Ch 1, turn, sc2tog, sc in next 5 sts. (6 sc)

Row 30: Ch 1, turn, sc in next 5 sts, 2 sc in next st. (7 sc)

Row 31: Ch 1, turn, 2 sc in next st, sc in next 6 sts. (8 sc)

Row 32: Ch 1, turn, sc2tog, sc in next 6 sts. (7 sc)

Row 33: Ch 1, turn, sc in next 5 sts, sc2tog. (6 sc)

Row 34: Ch 1, turn, (sc2tog) 2 times, sc in next 2 sts. (4 sts)

Sl st to last st of Row 33.

Fasten off. Do not fasten off on second one.

Cloud Assembly
Rnd 1: Place WS together, ch 1, working through both panels, sl st around cloud panels; join with sl st to first sl st. Fasten off.

Raindrop (make 1 each in B, C, and D)
Front
Ch 2.

Row 1 (RS): 2 sc in second ch from hook. (2 sc)

Row 2: Ch 1, turn, sc in each st. (2 sc)

Row 3: Ch 1, turn, 2 sc in first st, 2 sc in next st. (4 sc)

Row 4: Ch 1, turn, 2 sc in first st, sc in next 2 sts, 2 sc in next st. (6 sc)

Rows 5–6: Ch 1, turn, sc in each st across.

Row 7: Ch 1, turn, sc2tog, sc in next 2 sts, sc2tog. (4 sts)

Fasten off.

Back
Ch 2.

Rows 1–7: Rep front panel.

Row 8: Place WS of front and back panels together; working through both panels, ch 1, turn, sc2tog 2 times, sc evenly around 2 sides of raindrop panels with (sc, ch 1, sc) in top of Row 1; join with sl st to sc.

Fasten off.

Joining Raindrops
Join coordinating color as raindrop, ch 4; join with sl st to bottom of cloud. Weave in ends. Rep for each raindrop.

Strap 1
With B, ch 7.

Row 1 (RS): Sc in second ch from hook and in each across. (6 sc)

Rows 2–5: Ch 1, turn, sc in each st across.

Fasten off, leaving a long tail for sewing.

Sew the middle of strap 1 on back of cloud.

Strap 2
With B, ch 46.

Row 1 (RS): Sc in second ch from hook and in each across. (45 sc)

Rows 2–4: Ch 1, turn, sc in each st across.

Fasten off.

Put Velcro on each end of strap 2.

Slip strap 2 through strap 1. Join strap with Velcro over baby car seat handle.

Modern Flair Rug

Whether you're up late changing diapers or playing on the floor, keep those floors warm with a colorful and textured rug.

Yarn

Bernat Maker Home Dec; super bulky weight #5; 72% cotton, 28% nylon; 8.8 oz (250 g)/317 yds (290 m)

- 1 skein: 11009 Cream (**A**)
- 2 skeins: 11005 Aqua (**B**)

Hook and Other Materials

- US size M/N-13 (9 mm) crochet hook
- Yarn needle

Finished Measurements

44 in (112 cm) wide x 17 in (43 cm) long

Gauge

5 sc x 6 rows = 2 in (5 cm)
Adjust hook size if necessary to obtain gauge.

Special Stitch

Bobble: Yarn over 2 times, insert hook into next stitch, yarn over, pull back through, yarn over, pull through 2 loops, yarn over, pull through 2 loops, * yarn over 2 times, insert hook into same stitch, yarn over, pull back through, yarn over, pull through 2 loops, yarn over, pull through 2 loops, rep from * one more time, yarn over, pull through all loops on hook to complete.

Pattern Notes

- Weave in ends as work progresses.
- The beginning ch-2 will not count as a stitch unless otherwise stated.
- For a photo tutorial on working into the back loop (BLO) and front loop (FLO), see page 162.

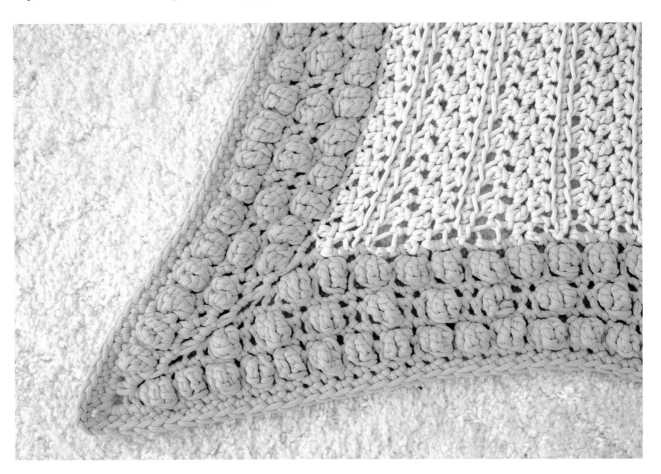

INSTRUCTIONS

Middle Section

With A, ch 46.

Row 1 (RS): Sc in 2nd chain from hook, *sc in next ch, dc in next chain; rep from * across. (45 sts)

Row 2: Ch 1, turn, sc in first st, *sc in next st, dc in next st; rep from * across.

Row 3: Ch 1, turn, working in the BLO, sc in each st across.

Row 4: Ch 1, turn, working in the FLO, sc in first st, *sc in next st, dc in next st; rep from * across.

Rows 5–6: Ch 1, turn, sc in first st, *sc in next st, dc in next st; rep from * across.

Rows 7–21: Rep Rows 3–6, ending on Row 5.
Fasten off.

Border

Rnd 1 (RS): With RS facing, join B in top right corner, ch 1, (2 sc, ch 3, 2 sc) in first st, sc in next 43 sts, (2 sc, ch 3, 2 sc) in last st, work 21 sc evenly across edge, (2 sc, ch 3, 2 sc) in first st of Row 1, sc in next 43 sts, (2 sc, ch 3, 2 sc) in last st, work 21 sc evenly across edge; join with sl st to first sc. (144 sts, 4 ch-3 sps)

Rnd 2: Sl st in next st, sl st in ch-3 sp, ch 1, (2 sc, ch 3, 2 sc) in same sp, sc in next st, [Bobble in next st, sc in next st] across to last st, (2 sc, ch 3, 2 sc) in last st, sc in next st, [Bobble in next st, sc in next st] across to last st, (2 sc, ch 3, 2 sc) in first st of Row 1, sc in next st, [Bobble in next st, sc in next st] across to last st, (2 sc, ch 3, 2 sc) in last st, sc in next st, [Bobble in next st, sc in next st] across to last st; join with sl st in first sc. (160 sts, 4 ch-3 sps)

Rnd 3: Sl st in next st, sl st in ch-3 sp, ch 1, sc in each sc around with (2 sc, ch 3, 2 sc) in each ch-3 sp; join with sl st to first sc. (176 sts, 4 ch-3 sps)

Rnd 4: Rep Rnd 2. (192 sts, 4 ch-3 sps)

Rnd 5: Rep Rnd 3. (208 sts, 4 ch-3 sps)

Rnd 6: Rep Rnd 2. (224 sts, 4 ch-3 sps)

Rnd 7: Rep Rnd 3. (240 sts, 4 ch-3 sps)

Rnd 8: Rep Rnd 3. (256 sts, 4 ch-3 sps)
Fasten off. Weave in ends.

Cloth and Towel

Milk bottle spill? Check. Baby spit-up? Check. Messes are inevitable! Have a few crocheted cloths and towels on hand to make cleaning up a breeze!

Yarn

Willow Yarns Meadow; medium weight #4; 100% cotton; 1.75 oz (50 g)/103 yds (95 m) per skein
- 3 skeins: 0001 White (**A**)
- 2 skeins each: 0009 Spruce (**B**), 0026 Daylily (**C**)

Hook and Other Materials
- US size G-6 (4 mm) crochet hook
- Yarn needle

Finished Measurements

Cloth: Approximately 9½ in x 11½ in (25 cm x 29 cm)

Towel: Approximately 14 in x 18 in (35.5 cm x 45.7 cm)

Gauge

16 sts in Row 2 pattern = 4 in (10.2 cm)
Adjust hook size if necessary to obtain gauge.

Pattern Note

When changing colors, complete the stitch before the color change until the last pull-through; drop working yarn, pull through next color as last pull-through to complete color change, and finish stitch. See photo tutorial on page 174.

INSTRUCTIONS

Cloth

With A, ch 41.

Row 1 (WS): Sl st in 3rd ch from hook, *hdc in next ch, sl st in next ch; rep from * across, ending with sl st in last ch.

Row 2 (RS): Ch 2 (counts as first hdc), turn, *sl st in next st, hdc in next st; rep from * across, ending with hdc in last st.

Rows 3–4: Rep Row 2. Join B, fasten off A.

Rows 5–8: Rep Row 2. Join C, fasten off B.

Rows 9–12: Rep Row 2. Join A, fasten off C.
Rows 13–16: Rep Row 2. Join B, fasten off A.
Rows 17–48: Rep Rows 5–16, ending on Row 12. Do not fasten off.

Trim
Rnd 1: Ch 1, turn, *3 sc in first st, sc in each st across to last st, 3 sc in last st, sc evenly across edge**, 3 sc in first st on Row 1; rep from * across, ending rep at **; join with sl st to first sc.

Towel
With A, ch 61.
Row 1 (RS): Sl st in 3rd ch from hook, *hdc in next ch, sl st in next ch; rep from * across, ending with sl st in last ch.
Row 2: Ch 2 (counts as first hdc), turn, *sl st in next st; hdc in next st; rep from * across, ending with hdc in last st. Join B, fasten off A.
Rows 3–4: Rep Row 2. Join A, fasten off B.
Rows 5–6: Rep Row 2. Join C, fasten off A.
Rows 7–8: Rep Row 2. Join A, fasten off C.
Rows 9–10: Rep Row 2. Join B, fasten off A.
Rows 11–20: Rep Rows 3–10, ending on Row 4.
Rows 21–73: Rep Row 2.
Do not fasten off.

Trim
Rnd 1: Ch 1, *sc evenly across edge, 3 sc in first st on Row 1, sc in each st across to last st, 3 sc in last st **; rep from * across, ending rep at **; join with sl st to first sc.

Pocket Wall Hanging

When my twins were li'l babies, I had a little toy train that I would hand them while I was changing their diapers. It kept them occupied, and they would look for it every single time! I kept it in the same place, and they knew where it was. This pocket wall hanging would be the perfect place for that sweet toy or things you need to keep close by, such as little lotions or wipe packs. Personalize and utilize your decor for your needs.

Yarn

Cascade Yarns Aegean Tweed; light weight #3; 100% organic wool; 3.5 oz (100 g)/328 yds (300 m) per skein
- 1 skein each: 11 Pesto (**A**), 07 Cream (**B**), 22 Marine (**C**)

Hook and Other Materials
- US size G-6 (4 mm) crochet hook
- Yarn needle
- 12 in (30.5 cm) dowel rod

Finished Measurements

7 in (18 cm) wide x 18 in (45.7 cm) long

Gauge

15 dc = 4 in (10.2 cm)
Adjust hook size if necessary to obtain gauge.

Special Stitch

3-Double Crochet Cluster (3-dc cl): Yarn over, insert hook in st, yarn over, pull through st, yarn over, pull through 2 loops on hook, (yarn over, insert hook in same st, yarn over, pull through st, yarn over, pull through 2 loops on hook) 3 times, yarn over, pull through all 5 loops on hook.

Pattern Notes
- When changing colors, complete the stitch before the color change until the last pull-through; drop working yarn, pull through next color as last pull-through to complete color change, and finish stitch. See photo tutorial on page 174.
- The beginning ch-2 of a round will not count as a stitch unless otherwise indicated.
- The beginning ch-3 counts as first dc.
- The beginning ch-4 counts as first dc plus ch-1.

INSTRUCTIONS

Motif (make 2)

With A, ch 5; join with sl st to first ch to form a ring.

Rnd 1 (RS): Ch 4 (counts as first dc and ch-1), (dc, ch 1) in ring 11 times; join with sl st to ch-3 of beg ch-4. (12 dc, 12 ch-1 sps) Fasten off.

Rnd 2: Join B in ch-1 sp, ch 4, dc in same sp, *sk next dc, (dc, ch 1, dc) in next ch-sp; rep from * around; join with sl st to ch-3 of beg ch-4. (24 dc, 12 ch-2 sps) Fasten off.

Rnd 3: Join C in ch-1 sp, ch 2, 3-dc cl in next ch-1 sp, ch 4, sk next 2 dc, *3-dc cl, ch 4, sk next 2 dc; rep from * around; join with sl st to first cluster. (12 cl, 12 ch-4 sps) Fasten off.

Rnd 4: Join A in ch-4 sp, ch 3, 4 dc in same sp, sk next cl, *5 dc in next ch-sp, sk next cl; rep from * around; join with sl st to beg ch-3. (60 dc)

Rnd 5: Ch 3 (counts as first dc), dc in next st, hdc in next 3 sts, sc in next 4 sts, hdc in next st, dc in next 2 sts, (dc, ch 2, dc) in next st, *dc in next 2 sts, hdc in next 3 sts, sc in next 4 sts, hdc in next 3 sts, dc in next 2 sts, (dc, ch 2, dc) in next st; rep from * around; join with sl st to beg ch-3. (4 ch-2 sps, 64 sts)

Rnd 6: Ch 3 (counts as first dc), dc in next 14 sts, (dc, ch 2, dc) in next ch-2 sp, *dc in next 16 sts, (dc, ch 2, dc) in next ch-2 sp; rep from * to last ch-2 sp, dc in next dc; join with sl st to beg ch-3. (72 sts, 4 ch-2 sps) Fasten off.

Rnd 7: Join C in ch-2 sp, ch 4, dc in same sp, (ch 1, sk 1, 3-dc cl in next st) 9 times, *(dc, ch 2, dc) in ch-2 sp, (ch 1, sk 1, 3-dc cl in next st) 9 times; rep from * around; join with sl st to ch-3 of beg ch-4. [9 ch-1, 9 cl on each side, 4 (dc, ch 2, dc) groups in corner] Fasten off.

Rnd 8: Join A in ch-2 sp, ch 3, 2 dc in same sp, *dc in next dc, dc in each ch-1 sp and cl, dc in next dc (20 dc), 5 dc in next ch-2 sp, rep from * around, ending with 2 dc in beg ch-2 sp; join with sl st to beg ch-3. (100 sts) Fasten off.

Back Panel

With B, ch 31.

Row 1 (RS): Sc in 2nd ch from hook and in each ch across. (30 sc)

Row 2: Ch 3, turn, dc in each st across.

Row 3: Ch 1, turn, sc in each st across.

Rows 4–57: Rep Rows 2 and 3.

Fasten off.

Finishing

Use yarn needle and sew each motif onto back panel, leaving the top side open to create a pocket.

Use yarn needle to sew back panel onto dowel rod.

Cut fifty 14-in (35.5-cm) lengths and, using 10 strands, add as fringe 5 times along edge evenly. Trim evenly at 7 in (17.8 cm).

Ring Stacker

Keep older siblings busy with this ring stacker! Each ring is smaller than the last and will keep them intrigued while you tend to the baby. Or they might throw the rings like frisbees and bonk you with the cone. Whatever keeps them busy!

Yarn

Berroco Ultra Wool; medium weight #4; 100% superwash wool; 3.5 oz (100 g)/219 yds (200 m) per skein

- 1 skein each: 3328 Bittersweet (**A**), 3316 Thyme (**B**), 3325 Delicata (**C**), 3301 Cream (**D**)

Hook and Other Materials

- US size G-6 (4 mm) crochet hook
- Yarn needle
- 8 in x 11 in (20.5 cm x 28 cm) sheet of cardstock
- Hot glue gun and glue sticks
- Poly-Fil stuffing
- Cardboard
- Stitch markers

Finished Measurements

11 in (28 cm) high x 6 in (15.2 cm) wide at base

Gauge

14 sc x 16 rows = 4 in (10.2 cm)
Adjust hook size if necessary to obtain gauge.

Pattern Notes

- The cone is made in 2 pieces: cone and cone base.
- The rings are made in continuous rounds and joined to complete.

INSTRUCTIONS

Cone

With A, ch 2.

Rnd 1 (RS): Work 3 sc in 2nd ch from hook, work in continuous rnds (spiral). (3 sc)

Note: Place marker in last sc made to indicate end of rnd. Move marker up as each rnd is completed.

Rnd 2: Work 2 sc in each sc around. (6 sc)

Rnd 3: *2 sc in next st, sc in next 2 sts; rep from * around. (8 sc)

Rnd 4: Sc in each st around. (8 sc)

Rnd 5: *2 sc in next st, sc in next 3 sts; rep from * around. (10 sc)

Rnd 6: Sc in each st around.

Rnd 7: *2 sc in next st, sc in next 4 sts; rep from * around. (12 sc)

Rnd 8: Sc in each st around.

Rnd 9: *2 sc in next st, sc in next 5 sts; rep from * around. (14 sc)

Rnd 10: Sc in each st around.

Rnd 11: *2 sc in next st, sc in next 6 sts; rep from * around. (16 sc)

Rnd 12: Sc in each st around.

Rnd 13: *2 sc in next st, sc in next 7 sts; rep from * around. (18 sc)

Rnd 14: Sc in each st around.
Rnd 15: *2 sc in next st, sc in next 8 sts; rep from * around. (20 sc)
Rnd 16: Sc in each st around.
Rnd 17: *2 sc in next st, sc in next 9 sts; rep from * around. (22 sc)
Rnd 18: Sc in each st around.
Rnd 19: *2 sc in next st, sc in next 10 sts; rep from * around. (24 sc)
Rnd 20: Sc in each st around.
Rnd 21: *2 sc in next st, sc in next 11 sts; rep from * around. (26 sc)
Rnd 22: Sc in each st around.
Rnd 23: *2 sc in next st, sc in next 12 sts; rep from * around. (28 sc)
Rnd 24: Sc in each st around.
Rnd 25: *2 sc in next st, sc in next 13 sts; rep from * around. (30 sc)
Rnd 26: Sc in each st around.
Rnd 27: *2 sc in next st, sc in next 14 sts; rep from * around. (32 sc)
Rnd 28: Sc in each st around.

Rnd 29: *2 sc in next st, sc in next 15 sts; rep from * around. (34 sc)
Rnd 30: Sc in each st around.
Rnd 31: *2 sc in next st, sc in next 16 sts; rep from * around. (36 sc)
Rnd 32: Sc in each st around.
Rnd 33: *2 sc in next st, sc in next 17 sts; rep from * around. (38 sc)
Rnd 34: Sc in each st around.
Rnd 35: *2 sc in next st, sc in next 18 sts; rep from * around. (40 sc)
Rnd 36: Sc in each st around.
Rnd 37: *2 sc in next st, sc in next 19 sts; rep from * around. (42 sc)
Rnd 38: Sc in each st around.
Rnd 39: *2 sc in next st, sc in next 20 sts; rep from * around. (44 sc)
Rnd 40: Sc in each st around.
Rnd 41: *2 sc in next st, sc in next 21 sts; rep from * around. (46 sc)
Rnd 42: Sc in each st around.
Rnd 43: *2 sc in next st, sc in next 22 sts; rep from * around. (48 sc)
Rnd 44: Sc in each st around.
Rnd 45: *2 sc in next st, sc in next 23 sts; rep from * around. (50 sc)
Rnd 46: Sc in each st around.
Rnd 47: *2 sc in next st, sc in next 24 sts; rep from * around. (52 sc)
Rnd 48: Sc in each st around.
Rnd 49: *2 sc in next st, sc in next 25 sts; rep from * around. (54 sc)
Rnd 50: Sc in each st around.
Fasten off, leaving a long tail for sewing.
Roll cardstock into a cone. Insert into crocheted cone and mark where edges meet. Pull cardstock out of cone and hot glue into a cone shape. Hot glue crocheted cone over cardstock form.

Cone Base
With A, ch 2.
Rnd 1 (RS): Work 6 sc in 2nd ch from hook, work in continuous rnds (spiral). (6 sc)
Note: Place marker in last sc made to indicate end of rnd. Move marker up as each rnd is completed.
Rnd 2: Work 2 sc in each sc around. (12 sc)
Rnd 3: *2 sc in next st, sc in next st; rep from * around. (18 sc)
Rnd 4: *Sc in next 2 sts, 2 sc in next st; rep from * around. (24 sc)

Rnd 5: *Sc in next 3 sts, 2 sc in next st; rep from *
around. (30 sc)

Rnd 6: *Sc in next 4 sts, 2 sc in next st; rep from *
around. (36 sc)

Rnd 7: *Sc in next 5 sts, 2 sc in next st; rep from *
around. (42 sc)

Rnd 8: *Sc in next 6 sts, 2 sc in next st; rep from *
around. (48 sc)

Rnd 9: *Sc in next 7 sts, 2 sc in next st; rep from *
around. (54 sc)

Using the cone base as a template, cut circle from
cardboard.

Stuff cone with Poly-Fil stuffing and sew cone base
onto cone, inserting cardboard.

Rings

Ring 1 (Bottom Ring)

With B, ch 14, join with sl st to first sc.

Rnd 1 (RS): Ch 1, sc in each ch around; work in
continuous rnds (spiral). (14 sc)

*Note: Place marker in last sc made to indicate
end of rnd. Move marker up as each rnd is
completed.*

Rnds 2–approx. 67: Sc in each st around until piece
measures approx. 13½ in (34.3 cm). Stuff as you
go.

Fasten off, leaving a long tail for sewing.
Stuff firmly before sewing ends together.
Thread yarn needle with long tail, and sew ends
together.

Ring 2

With C, work as for Ring 1 through approx. Rnd 62,
until piece measures 12½ in (31.8 cm).

Ring 3

With A, work as for Ring 1 through approx. Rnd 58,
until piece measures 11 in (28 cm).

Ring 4

With D, work as for Ring 1 through approx. Rnd 53,
until piece measures 10 in (25.4 cm).

Ring 5

With B, work as for Ring 1 through approx. Rnd 44,
until piece measures 9 in (22.9 cm).

Eden Sampler Blanket

Designed for comfort and beauty, this blanket will be a pleasure to crochet. Made in a stitch-sampler style, each round is new and interesting. Mix and match colors as you crochet a blanket heirloom for you and your baby!

Yarn

Willow Yarns Meadow; worsted weight #4; 100% cotton; 1.75 oz (50 g)/103 yds (95 m) per skein
- 5 skeins: 0007 Brush (**A**)
- 2 skeins each: 0001 White (**B**), 0006 Succulent (**C**), 0019 Pebble (**E**)
- 1 skein: 0008 Leaf (**D**)

Hook and Other Materials

- US size H-8 (5 mm) crochet hook
- Yarn needle

Finished Measurements

35 in x 35 in (89 x 89 cm)

Gauge

Rnds 1–6 = 4 in (10.2 cm)
Adjust hook size if necessary to obtain gauge.

Special Stitches

Back Post Slip Stitch (BPsl st): Insert hook from back to front to back around post of st indicated, yarn over and pull up loop, draw through loop on hook.

Beginning Cluster (Beg cl): Ch 2, yarn over and insert hook in same st and draw up a loop, yarn over and draw through 2 loops on hook, yarn over and draw through all loops on hook.

2-Double Crochet Cluster (2-dc cl): Yarn over, insert hook in next, yarn over, pull up loop, yarn over, pull through 2 loops, yarn over, insert hook in same st, yarn over, pull up a loop, yarn over, pull through 2 loops, yarn over, pull through all loops on hook.

Beginning Front Post Cluster (beg FPcl): Insert hook from front to back to front around post of st indicated, ch 2, yarn over and insert hook in same st and draw up a loop, yarn over and draw through 2 loops on hook, yarn over and draw through all loops on hook.

Front Post 2-Double Crochet Cluster (FPcl): Yarn over, insert hook from front to back to front around post of st indicated, yarn over, pull up loop, yarn over, pull through 2 loops, yarn over, insert hook on same post, yarn over, pull up loop, yarn over, pull through 2 loops, yarn over, pull through all loops on hook.

4-Double Crochet Cluster (4-dc cl): Yarn over, insert hook in next, yarn over, pull up loop, yarn over, pull through 2 loops, (yarn over insert hook in same st, yarn over, pull up a loop, yarn over, pull through 2 loops) 3 times, yarn over, pull through all loops on hook.

Front Post Treble Crochet (FPtr): Yarn over 2 times, insert hook from front to back to front around post of st indicated, yarn over and pull up a loop, (yarn over and draw through 2 loops on hook) 3 times. See photo tutorial on page 172.

Back Post Single Crochet (BPsc): Insert hook from back to front to back around post of st indicated, yarn over and pull up a loop, yarn over and draw through 2 loops on hook. See photo tutorial on working into stitch posts on page 170.

Pattern Notes
- Beginning ch-3 counts as first dc.
- Beginning ch-4 counts as first dc and ch-1 or first tr. Each round will specify as needed.
- For instructions on working into stitch posts and back loop (BLO), see photo tutorials on pages 170 and 162.

INSTRUCTIONS

With A, ch 5, join to first ch to form ring.

Rnd 1 (RS): Ch 1, 8 sc in ring, join. (8 sc) Fasten off.

Rnd 2: Join B in any st, (ch 3, tr, ch 3, sl st) in same st, (sl st, ch 3, tr, ch 3, sl st) in each st around st; join with sl st to beg ch-3. (8 petals) Fasten off.

Rnd 3: Join A in back of tr in any petal, ch 3, *BPsl st in next tr of next petal, ch 3; rep from * around; join with sl st to first BPsl st. (8 BPsl st, 8 ch-3 sp)

Rnd 4: Ch 1, *[sc in next ch-sp, (tr between 2 sl sts between petals on Round 2, sc in same ch-sp) 2 times]; rep from * around; join with a sl st to first sc. (32 sc, 16 tr) Fasten off.

Rnd 5: Join C in sc between tr in BLO, ch 1, working in BLO, sc in each st around; join with sl st to first sc. (48 sc) Fasten off.

Rnd 6: Join B in first sc, (beg cl, ch 3, 2-dc cl) in same, sk 3, *(2-dc cl, ch 3, 2-dc cl) in next, ch 3; rep from * around; join with a sl st to beg cl. [12 (2-dc cl, ch 3, 2-dc cl) groups]

Rnd 7: Sl st to next ch-3 sp, ch 3, 4 dc in same sp, sk 1 cl, sc in sp between next cl and skipped cl, sk 1 cl, *5 dc in next ch-3 sp, sk 1 cl, sc in sp between next cl and skipped cl, sk 1 cl; rep from * around; join with sl st to beg ch-3. (12 5-dc groups, 12 sc) Fasten off.

Rnd 8: Join D in any sc with beg FPcl, ch 2, sk 2 dc, BPsl st on next st, ch 2, sk 2 dc, *FPcl on next sc, ch 2, sk 2 dc, BPsl st on next st, ch 2, sk 2 dc; rep from * around; join with sl st to beg FPcl. (12 FPcl, 12 BPsl st, 24 ch-2 sp) Fasten off.

Rnd 9: Join E, sl st to next ch-sp, ch 1, (sc, hdc, 2 dc) in same sp, dc in next BPsl st, (2 dc, hdc, sc) in next ch-sp, sk 1 cl, *(sc, hdc, 2 dc) in next ch-sp, dc in next BPsl st, (2 dc, hdc, sc) in next ch-sp, sk 1 cl; rep from * around; join with sl st to first sc. (108 sts)

Rnd 10: Ch 1, sc in first st, ch 8, sk 2 sts, sc in next st, *sc in next st, ch 8, sk 2 sts, sc in next st; rep from * around; join with sl st to first sc. (27 ch-8 loops, 54 sc)

Rnd 11: Ch 1, sk 1 sc, *(sl st, sc 4, ch 2, sc 4, sl st) in next ch-8 sp, sk 2 sc; rep from * around, ending with sk 1 sc; join with sl st to first sl st. [27 (sl st, sc 4, ch 2, sc 4, sl st) groups] Fasten off.

Rnd 12: Join A in any ch-2 sp, ch 3 (counts as dc), 4 dc in same sp, 5 dc in each ch-2 sp in middle of each group around; join with sl st to beg ch-3. (135 dc) Fasten off.

Rnd 13: Join B in any st in BLO, working in BLO, sc in each st around; join with sl st to first sc. (135 sc) Fasten off.

Rnd 14: Join D in any st, ch 1, *sc, ch 2, sk 1 st; rep from * around to last st, ending with sc in last st, ch 2; join with sl st to first sc. (68 sc, 68 ch-2) Fasten off.

Rnd 15: Join C in first skipped sc on Round 13, ch 4 (counts as dc and ch-1), working over ch, dc in same sp, sk 1 sc, *working over ch, (dc, ch 1, dc) in skipped sc on Round 13, sk 1; rep from * around, working last (dc, ch 1, dc) in sp between last and first sc on Round 14; join with sl st to ch-3 of beg ch-4. [68 (dc, ch 1, dc) groups] Fasten off.

Rnd 16: Join B in ch-1 sp, (beg cl, ch 3, cl, ch 3, 2-dc cl) in same sp, sk next 2 (dc, ch 1, dc), sl st in space between last skipped dc and next, sk 1 dc, *(2-dc cl, ch 3, 2-dc cl, ch 3, 2-dc cl) in next ch-1 sp, sk next 2 (dc, ch 1, dc), sl st in space between last skipped dc and next, sk 1 dc; rep from * around; join with a sl st to beg cl. [34 sl st, 34 (2-dc cl, ch 3, 2-dc cl) groups] Fasten off.

Rnd 17: Join E in next ch-3 sp, ch 3, 2 dc in same sp, 3 dc in each ch-sp around; join with sl st to beg ch-3. (204 dc) Fasten off.

Note: The blanket will be wavy at this point, but it will even out.

Rnd 18: Join D in BLO, ch 1, working in BLO, sc in each st around; join with sl st to first sc. (204 sc) Fasten off.

Rnd 19: Join A in any st, ch 3, dc in next 3 sts, ch 3, sk 3 sts, dc in next 4 sts, ch 1, sc in next 40 sts, ch 1, *dc in next 4 sts, ch 3, sk 3 sts, dc in next 4 sts, ch 1, sc in next 40 sts, ch 1; rep from * around; join with sl st to beg ch-3. (24 dc, 4 ch-3 sp, 160 sc) Fasten off.

Rnd 20: Join C in ch-1 space to right of corner, ch 2 (not a st), dc in same sp, *ch 2, sk 4 dc, 11 tr in ch-3 sp, ch 2, sk 4 dc, dc in ch-1 sp, (sk 1, dc in next, dc in skipped) 20 times**, dc in ch-1 sp; rep from * around, ending last rep at **; join with sl st to first dc. (8 ch-2, 44 tr, 168 dc) Fasten off.

Rnd 21: Join B in ch-2 sp to right of corner, ch 3 (not a st), 2 tr in same, *ch 5, 4-dc cl in 2nd skipped sc on Round 19, ch 5, 2 tr in next ch-2 on Round 20, tr in next 5 sts, dc in next 5 sts, sc in next 22 sts, dc in next 5 sts, tr in next 5 sts**, 2 tr in next ch-2 sp; rep from * around, ending last rep at **; join with sl st to first tr. (56 tr, 40 dc, 88 sc, 8 ch-5, 4 4-dc cl) Fasten off.

Rnd 22: Join E in ch-5 sp to right of corner, ch 4 (counts as first tr), tr in same sp, *sk next 5 tr on Rnd 20, [tr, (ch 1, tr) 6 times] in next, 2 tr in next ch-5 of Rnd 21, (ch 1, sk 1, 2-dc cl in next st) 23 times**, 2 tr in next ch-5 sp; rep from * around, ending last repeat at **; join with sl st to beg ch-4. [(16 tr, 23 2-dc cl, 23 ch-1 sp, 1 corner) per side] Fasten off.

Rnd 23: Join A in 4th tr in corner, ch 3 (counts as dc), 2 dc in same st, *(dc in next ch-1 sp, dc in next tr) 3 times, dc in next 2 tr, (dc in next ch-1 sp, dc in next cl) 23 times, dc in next 3 tr, (dc in next ch-1, dc in next tr) 2 times, dc in next ch-1 sp**, 3 dc in next tr; rep from * around, ending last repeat at **; join with sl st to beg ch-3. (260 dc) Fasten off.

Rnd 24: Join C in 2nd dc in corner, ch 4, 2 tr in same st, *(sk 2 sts, tr in next 2 sts, working in front, tr in skipped 2 sts) 16 times**, 3 dc in corner; rep from * around, ending last repeat at **; join with sl st to beg ch-4. (268 sts) Do not fasten off.

Rnd 25: Sl st to next tr, ch 4 (counts as tr), 2 tr in same st, *tr in next st, FPtr on next 2 sts, (sk 2 sts, FPtr on next 2 sts, working behind 2 tr made, FPtr on next skipped 2 sts) 15 times, FPtr on next 2 sts, tr in next sts**, 3 tr in next st; rep from * around, ending last repeat at **; join with sl st to beg ch-4. (276 sts)

Rnd 26: Sl st to next st, ch 4 (counts as tr), 2 tr in same st, *tr in next 2 sts, (sk 2 sts, FPtr on next 2 sts, working in front, FPtr on skipped 2 sts) 16 times, tr in next 2 sts**, 3 tr in next sts; rep from * around, ending last repeat at **; join with sl st to beg ch-4. (284 sts) Fasten off.

Rnd 27: Join B in 2nd tr in corner, ch 3 (counts as first dc), 2 dc in same st, dc in next 70 sts, *3 dc in next st, dc in next 70 sts; rep from * around; join with sl st to beg ch-3. (292 dc) Fasten off.

Rnd 28: Join D in 2nd dc in corner, ch 1, 3 sc in same st, (sc in next st, ch 3, sk 2 sts) 24 times, *3 sc in next st, (sc in next st, ch 3, sk 2 sts) 24 times; rep from * around; join with sl st to first sc. [96 (sc, ch 3, sk 2) groups, 4 3-sc corners] Fasten off.

Rnd 29: Join E in first sc (after the group of 3 sc in corner), ch 1, sc in same st, *[(dc, ch 1, dc, ch 1, dc) in next ch-3 sp, sc in next sc] 24 times, (dc, ch 1, dc, ch 1, dc) in next sc (corner made), sk next sc**, sc in next; rep from * around, ending last repeat at **; join with sl st to first sc. [100 (dc, ch 1, dc, ch 1, dc) groups, 100 sc] Fasten off.

Rnd 30: Join A in sc to left of corner, ch 4 (counts as first dc and ch-1), *(sk 1 dc, sk 1 ch-1 sp, BPsc in next st, ch 1, sk 1 ch-1 sp, sk 1 dc, dc in next sc, ch 1) 24 times, ch 1, sk 1 dc, sk ch-1 sp, 3 dc in next, ch 1, sk ch-1, sk dc**, dc in next; rep from * around, ending last repeat at**; join with sl st to beg ch-4. [(25 dc, 24 BPsc, 50 ch-1 sp) on each side, 3 dc in each corner] Fasten off.

Rnd 31: Join A in first dc, ch 3, *(dc in next ch-1, dc in next st) across to 2nd dc in corner, 3 dc in 2nd dc in corner; rep from * around, dc in next, dc in next ch-1; join with sl st to beg ch-3. (101 dc on each side, 3 dc in each corner)

Rnd 32: Ch 1, sc in each st around with 3 sc in 2nd dc in each corner; join with sl st to first sc. (432 sc) Fasten off.

Rnd 33: Join A in 2nd sc in corner, ch 3, 2 dc in same st, *(dc in next 2 sts, dc around 2 dc posts just made, sk 1) 35 times**, 3 dc in next (corner); rep from * around, ending last rep at **; join with sl st to first dc. (140 wrapped sets, 4 3-dc corners)

Rnd 34: Ch 1, sc in each st around with 3 sc in 2nd dc in each corner; join with sl st to first sc. (440 sc)

Rnd 35: Ch 3, dc in each st with 3 dc in 2nd sc in each corner; join with sl st to beg ch-3. (448 dc) Fasten off.

Rnd 36: Join A in 2nd dc in corner, ch 3, 2 dc in same, dc in next st, *(ch 1, sk 1, dc in next st) 55 times**, 3 dc in next st, dc in next st; rep from * around, ending last rep at **; join with sl st to beg ch-3. (224 dc, 220 ch-1, 4 3-dc corners) Fasten off.

Rnd 37: Join A in 2nd dc in corner, ch 3, 2 dc in same st, dc in each st around with 3 dc in 2nd dc in each corner; join with sl st to beg ch-3. (464 dc) Fasten off.

Weave in ends.

Triangle Motif Garland

Decorate the baby shower or baby room with a fun garland. Make as many triangles in as many colors, and add a touch of softness to any space.

Yarn

Universal Cotton Supreme Sapling; bulky weight #5; 100% cotton; 3.5 oz (100 g)/109 yds (100 m) per skein
- 1 skein each: 815 Ecru (**A**), 812 Seafoam (**B**), 817 Brindle (**C**)

Hook and Other Materials

- US size J-10 (6 mm) crochet hook
- Yarn needle

Finished Measurements

Each completed triangle (with trim on 2 sides): 8 in (20 cm) wide x 7 in (18 cm) high

Gauge

Rnds 1–3 = 4 in (10.2 cm)
Adjust hook size if necessary to obtain gauge.

Pattern Notes

- The beginning ch-3 counts as first dc.
- This piece is meant to be used as decor only; be sure to keep it away from your baby.

INSTRUCTIONS

Triangles

Make 3 triangles with the following color sequence:
Rnd 1 (RS): A.
Rnd 2: A.
Rnd 3: A.
Rnd 4: B.
Rnd 5: C.
Make 2 panels with the following color sequence:
Rnd 1: B.
Rnd 2: B.
Rnd 3: B.

Rnd 4: A.
Rnd 5: C.

With first color (A or B), ch 4; join with sl st to first ch to form a ring.

Rnd 1: Ch 3, 2 dc in ring, ch 2, (3 dc in ring, ch 2) 2 times; join with sl st to beg ch-3. (9 dc, 3 ch-2 sps)

Rnd 2: Sl st to ch-2 sp, ch 3, (2 dc, ch 2, 3 dc) in same sp, ch 1, *(3 dc, ch 2, 3 dc) in next ch-2 sp, ch 2; rep from * around; join with sl st to beg ch-3. (18 dc, 3 ch-2 sps, 3 ch-1 sps)

Rnd 3: Sl st to ch-2 sp, ch 3, (2 dc, ch 2, 3 dc) in same sp, ch 1, sk 3 dc, 3 dc in next ch-1 sp, ch 1, sk 3 dc, *(3 dc, ch 2, 3 dc) in next ch-1 sp, ch 1, sk 3 dc, 3 dc in next ch-1 sp, ch 1, sk 3 dc; rep from * around. (27 dc, 6 ch-1 sps, 3 ch-2 sps) Fasten off.

Rnd 4: Join second color (B or A) in ch-2 sp, ch 3, (2 dc, ch 2, 3 dc) in same sp, ch 1, sk 3 dc, (3 dc in next ch-1 sp, ch 1, sk 3 dc) 2 times, *(3 dc, ch 2, 3 dc) in next ch-1 sp, ch 1, sk 3 dc, 3 dc in next ch-1 sp, ch 1, sk 3 dc; rep from * around. (36 dc, 9 ch-1 sps, 3 ch-2 sps) Fasten off.

Rnd 5: Join C in ch-2 sp, ch 1, 3 sc in same sp, sc in each dc and ch-1 sp across, *3 sc in next ch-2 sp, sc in each dc and ch-1 sp across; rep from * around; join with sl st to first st. Fasten off.

Joining

Lay triangles in preferred order.

With C, ch 25.

Row 1: Sc in triangle in 2nd sc in any corner, *sk 1 sc, 5 dc in next sc, (sk 1 sc, sc in next sc, sk 1 sc, 5 dc in next sc) 3 times, sk 2 sc, 5 dc in 2nd sc in next corner; rep from * across next edge to corner point, ending with sc in last corner; ch 8.

Rep Row 1 until each triangle is trimmed on 2 edges, ch 25. Fasten off.

Weave in ends.

Crib Caddy

This crib caddy makes for an adorable nursery storage basket. Toss in baby toys, pacifiers, and little stuffed animals, and clean up the nursery in a jiffy!

Yarn

Lion Brand Yarns Vel-Luxe Jumbo; jumbo weight #7; 100% polyester; 7 oz (200 g)/21 yds (19 m) per skein
- 3 skeins: 537-159 Mineral Yellow

Hook and Other Materials
- US size P/Q (15 mm) crochet hook
- Yarn needle

Finished Measurements
11½ in (29 cm) wide x 9 in (23 cm) high

Gauge
4 sc = 4 in (10.2 cm)
Adjust hook size if necessary to obtain gauge.

Special Stitch
Single Crochet 2 Together (sc2tog): (Insert hook, yarn over, pull up loop) in each of the stitches indicated, yarn over, draw through all loops on hook. See photo tutorial on page 167.

Pattern Notes
- When changing colors, complete the stitch before the color change until the last pull-through; drop working yarn, pull through next color as last pull-through to complete color change, and finish stitch. See photo tutorial on page 174.
- For photo tutorial on working into the back loop (BLO), see page 162.

INSTRUCTIONS

Ch 24; join with a sl st to first ch to create a ring—be sure not to twist the chain.

Rnd 1 (RS): Ch 1, sc in each ch around; join with sl st to first sc. (24 sc)

Rnds 2–4: Ch 1, working in the BLO, sc in each st around; join with sl st to first sc.

Rnds 5–9: Ch 1, sc in each st around; join with sl st to first sc.

Rnd 10: Ch 1, sc in next 5 sts, sc2tog, sc in next 10 sts, sc2tog; join with sl st to first sc. (22 sc)
Fasten off.
With WS facing, sew last row together to close bottom of basket.

Finishing

Cut 2 lengths of yarn 20 in (50.8 cm) long. Knot securely on back of caddy and tie on edge of crib.

Squishy Play Mat

This is the perfect mat for the nursery. Crocheted with jumbo yarn, it's super squishy and quick to make!

Yarn

Lion Brand Yarns, Vel-luxe Jumbo; jumbo weight #7; 100% polyester; 7 oz (200 g)/21 yds (19 m) per skein

- 2 skeins: 537-195 Cabaret (**A**)
- 3 skeins each: 537-142 Mulberry (**B**), 537-33 Golden Ochre (**C**)
- 1 skein: 537-149 Harbor Mist (**D**)

Hook and Other Materials

- US size P/Q (15 mm) crochet hook
- Yarn needle

Finished Measurements

20 in (50.8 cm) wide x 17 in (43 cm) high

Gauge

4 sc = 4 in (10.2 cm)
Adjust hook size if necessary to obtain gauge.

Pattern Notes

- When changing colors, complete the stitch before the color change until the last pull-through; drop working yarn, pull through next color as last pull-through to complete color change, and finish stitch. See photo tutorial on page 174.
- The beginning ch-3 counts as first dc.

INSTRUCTIONS

With A, ch 19.

Row 1 (RS): Sc in 2nd ch from hook and in each ch across. (18 sc) Fasten off.

Row 2: Join B, ch 3, turn, *sk 1 st, 2 dc in next st; rep from * across to last st, dc in last st. Fasten off.

Row 3: Join C, ch 3, turn, sk 1 dc, dc in sp between last skipped dc and next dc, *sk 2 dc, dc in sp between last skipped dc and next dc; rep from * across to to last 2 dc, sk 1 dc, dc in last. Fasten off.

Row 4: Join A. Rep Row 3. Fasten off.

Row 5: Join C. Rep Row 3. Fasten off.
Row 6: Join B. Rep Row 3. Fasten off.
Row 7: Join D. Rep Row 3. Fasten off.
Row 8: Join A. Rep Row 3. Fasten off.
Row 9: Join D. Rep Row 3. Fasten off.
Row 10: Join B. Rep Row 3. Fasten off.
Row 11: Join C. Rep Row 3. Fasten off.
Row 12: Join A. Rep Row 3. Fasten off.
Row 13: Join C. Rep Row 3. Fasten off.
Row 14: Join B. Rep Row 3. Fasten off.
Row 15: Join A, ch 1, sc in each st across. Fasten off.

Weave in ends.

Sensory Cube

Let the baby play! This creative sensory cube is sure to delight. Made with tabs, curlicues, textured yarn, and more, keep that cube rolling for hours of fun!

Yarn
Lion Brand Vanna's Choice; medium weight #4; 100% acrylic; 5 oz (141 g)/170 yds (156 m) per skein
- 1 skein each: 860-100 White (**A**), 860-110 Navy (**B**), 860-130 Honey (**C**), 860-158 Mustard (**D**), 860-150 Pale Grey (**E**)

Lion Brand Go for Faux; super bulky weight #6; 100% polyester; 3.5 oz (100 g)/65 yds (60 m) per skein
- 1 skein: 322-098 Baked Alaska (**F**)

Hooks and Other Materials
- US size H-8 (5 mm) and I-9 (5.5 mm) crochet hooks
- Yarn needle
- Six 8 in x 8 in (20 cm x 20 cm) plastic canvas squares
- Poly-Fil stuffing

Finished Measurements
8 in x 8 in (20 cm x 20 cm) cube

Gauge
With smaller hook and medium weight yarn, 16 sc = 4 in (10.2 cm)
Adjust hook size if necessary to obtain gauge.

Pattern Note
The cube is made by crocheting six 8 in x 8 in (20 cm x 20 cm) panels. Each panel has a special texture. Once each panel is complete, sew plastic canvas to the WS and then sew the completed squares together. Fill the cube with Poly-Fil stuffing before closing.

Textured circles and tabs

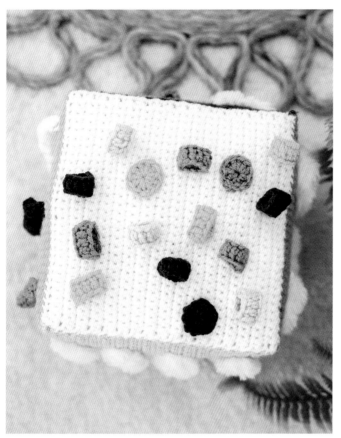

Tabs and circles

Top: tabs and circles; bottom: textured stripes

INSTRUCTIONS

Cube Panels
Crochet 2 squares in A and 1 square each in B, C, D, and E.
Ch 30.
Row 1 (WS): Sc in second ch from hook and in each ch across. (29 sc)
Rows 2–34: Ch 1, turn, sc in each st across.

Trim
Rnd 1 (RS): Ch 1, turn, working along ends of rows, sc 29, 3 sc in first st of Row 1, sc in next 27 sts, 3 sc in last st, working along ends of rows on next edge, sc 29, 3 sc in first st of Row 34, sc in next 27 sts, 3 sc in last st; join with sl st to first sc.
Fasten off.

Note: You can add any texture to any panel color.

Block 1: Curlicues (see page 92)
Make 3 curlicues in A, B, and C.
Ch 35.
Row 1: 2 dc in 3rd ch from hook, 3 dc in each ch across. (99 dc)
Fasten off.
Sew each end of curlicue to side of square. Also, secure each curlicue in the center and in 3 more other places. The curlicues are just for feeling, not pulling, so they need to be secure all along the length.

Block 2: Tabs and Circles
Tab
Create 3 tabs each in B, C, D, and E.
Ch 12.
Row 1: Dc in 4th ch from hook and in each ch across.
Fasten off, leaving a long tail for sewing.
Fold tab in half. Sew ends to the block in random order.

Fringe

Top: textured stripes; bottom: fringe

Circle
Make 1 circle each in B, C, and D.
Ch 4.
Rnd 1: 10 dc in first ch; join with sl st to first dc. (10 dc)
Fasten off.
Use yarn needle to sew circles in open spots around tabs.

Block 3: Fringe
Make 3 fringe sections by cutting 25 strands 6 in (15.2 cm) in length in B, C, and E.
Beginning on the 3rd row add the first row of fringe for each color fringe.
Adding fringe: Fold yarn in half. Pull center loop through a stitch, pull ends through center loop, pull tight.
Rep 10 rows apart.
Trim rows evenly.

Block 4: Textured Stripes
Make 4 textured stripes in F.
With F and larger hook, ch 10.
Row 1: Sc in 2nd ch from hook and in each ch across.
Fasten off, leaving a long tail for sewing.
Sew each stripe across block.

Block 5: Textured Circles and Tabs
Textured Circle
Make 3 textured circles in F.
With F and larger hook, ch 4.
Rnd 1: 7 dc in first ch; join with sl st to first dc.
Fasten off, leaving a long tail for sewing.

Textured Tab
Make 3 tabs (see Block 2) in A.
Use yarn needle and sew on the 3 circles and 3 tabs.

Block 6: Shapes

Square

With E, ch 11.

Row 1: Sc in second ch from hook and in each across. (10 sc)

Rows 2–10: Ch 1, turn, sc in each st across.

Trim: Ch 1, turn, 3 sc in first st, sc 8, 3 sc in last st, sc 10 evenly across end of rows, 3 sc in first st of Row 1, sc 8, 3 sc in next st, sc 10 evenly across second edge; join with sl st to first sc.

Fasten off, leaving a long tail for sewing.

Triangle

With C, ch 2.

Row 1: 2 sc in second ch from hook. (2 sc)

Row 2: Ch 1, turn, 2 sc in each st. (4 sc)

Row 3: Ch 1, turn, sc in each st across.

Row 4: Ch 1, turn, 2 sc in first st, sc in next 2 sts, 2 sc in last st. (6 sc)

Row 5: Rep Row 3.

Row 6: Ch 1, turn, 2 sc in first st, sc in next 4 sts, 2 sc in last st. (8 sc)

Row 7: Rep Row 3.

Row 8: Ch 1, turn, 2 sc in first st, sc in next 6 sts, 2 sc in last st. (10 sc)

Row 9: Rep Row 3.

Row 10: Ch 1, turn, 2 sc in first st, sc in next 8 sts, 2 sc in last st. (12 sts)

Row 11: Rep Row 3.

Row 12: Ch 1, turn, 2 sc in first st, sc in next 10 sts, 2 sc in last st. (14 sts)

Trim: Ch 1, turn, 3 sc in first st, sc in next 12 sts, 3 sc in last st, sc 12 evenly across ends of rows, 3 sc in top of Row 1, sc 12 evenly across ends of rows; join with sl st to first sc.

Fasten off, leaving a long tail for sewing.

Tab

Make 1 tab (see Block 2) in C.

Sew square and triangle on block.

Thread yarn needle with F and create an X in 2 open corners.

Sew on tab in random place.

Top: shapes; bottom: textured circles and tabs

Cube Assembly

Use yarn needle to sew plastic canvas to WS of each square. This will help hold the cube's structure.

Sew squares together through stitches, stuffing before closing.

Note: It is not required that you sew through the ends of the plastic canvas, but it will help keep the cube sturdy on the edges if the canvas is sewn through in at least a few stitches on each side.

Darling Flower Wreath

Don't forget the baby's door and walls! Add a simple touch of color and sweetness with this simple, yet elegant, flower wreath. It brings a breath of freshness to any space.

Yarn
Willow Yarns Meadow; medium weight #4; 100% cotton; 1.75 oz (50 g)/115 yds (105 m) per skein
- 1 skein each: 0016 Phlox (**A**), 0026 Daylily (**B**), 0002 Cream (**C**), 0010 Peacock (**D**), 0004 Nest (**E**), 0031 Windstorm (**F**), 0008 Leaf (**G**)

Hook and Other Materials
- US size H-8 (5 mm) crochet hook
- Yarn needle
- 10 in (25.5 cm) diameter wooden hoop
- Two 12-in (30.5-cm) felt panels
- Fabric glue
- Sewing needle and thread

Finished Measurements
10 in (25.5 cm) in diameter

Gauge
Exact gauge is not necessary for this project.

Special Stitches
Single Crochet 2 Together (sc2tog): (Insert hook, yarn over, pull up loop) in each of the stitches indicated, yarn over, draw through all loops on hook. See photo tutorial on page 167.

Double Crochet 2 Together (dc2tog): Yarn over, pull up a loop in next stitch, yarn over, pull through first 2 loops, yarn over, pull up a loop in the next stitch, yarn over and draw through first 2 loops, yarn over and pull through all loops on hook (counts as 1 dc). See photo tutorial on page 168.

Pattern Notes
- Create each flower and set aside. The wreath will be arranged at one time, after all flowers and leaves are complete.
- For photo tutorials on working into the back loop (BLO) and front loop (FLO), see page 162.

INSTRUCTIONS

Flower 1: Double Rolled Flower (make 2)
Back Flower
With A, ch 46.
Row 1 (RS): Dc in second ch from hook, (dc, ch 2, 2 dc) in same ch, sk 1 ch, sl st in next ch, *sk 1 ch, (2 dc, ch 2, 2 dc) in next ch, sk 1 ch, sl st in next st; rep from * across. (11 petals, 11 sl st) Fasten off, leaving a long tail for sewing.
Roll strip and sew together.

Front Flower

With B, Create a magic ring.

Rnd 1 (RS): Sc 6 in ring; join with sl st to first sc. (6 sc)

Rnd 2: Working in the FLO, (ch 3, sl st to next st in flo) around; do not join.

Rnd 3: (Sl st to next st in BLO, ch 3, sl st to same st, ch 3, sl st to same st) around.

Fasten off.

Sew front flower to back flower.

Flower 2: Lacy Rolled Flower (make 2)

With C, ch 51.

Row 1 (RS): (Sc, ch 2) in second ch from hook, (sc, ch 3) in next 11 chs, (dc, ch 2) in next 20 chs, (tr, ch 2) in next 18 chs.

Fasten off, leaving a long tail for sewing.

Roll strip and sew together.

Flower 3: Double-Layered Flower (make 3)

Back Flower

With D, ch 4; join with sl st to first ch.

Rnd 1 (RS): Ch 4 (counts as dc and ch 1), (dc, ch 1) 6 times in ring; join with sl st to ch-3 of beg ch-4. (7 dc, 7 ch-1 sps)

Rnd 2: (Sl st, ch 1, 3 dc, ch 1, sl st) in each ch-1 sp around. (7 petals)

Rnd 3: Sl st to skipped dc in Rnd 1 (between petals), *ch 3, sl st to next dc on Rnd 1 (after petal); rep from * around.

Rnd 4: (Sl st, ch 1, 5 dc, ch 1, sl st) in each ch-3 sp around.

Fasten off.

Front Flower

With E, ch 2.

Rnd 1 (RS): 5 sc in second ch from hook. (5 sc)

Rnd 2: (Sl st, ch 1, dc, ch 1, sl st) in each st around; join with sl st to first st.

Fasten off, leaving a long tail for sewing.

Sew front flower to back flower.

Flower 4: Large Middle Flower (make 1)

With B, ch 40.

Row 1 (RS): Dc in 4th ch from hook and in each across. (38 dc)

Row 2: Ch 1, turn, (sc, ch 1, sc) in each st across.

Row 3: Ch 1, turn, (sl st, ch 1, dc, tr, dc, ch 1, sl st) in each ch-1 sp across.

Fasten off, leaving a long tail for sewing.

Roll strip and sew together.

Flower 5: Mini Rolled Flower (make 1 in E and 3 in F)

Ch 31.

Row 1 (RS): Sc in second ch from hook, sc in next 5 chs, hdc in next 9 chs, dc in next 15 chs.

Fasten off, leaving a long tail for sewing.

Roll strip and sew together.

Leaves (make 4 in F and 6 in G)

Ch 9.

Row 1 (RS): Hdc in second ch from hook, dc in next st, 3 dc in next 3 chs, hdc in next ch, sc in next ch, 3 sc in last ch, working on opposite side of ch, sc in next st, hdc in next ch, 3 dc in next 3 sts, dc in next st, hdc in last st; join with sl st to first hdc. (29 sts)

Fasten off. Weave in ends.

Assembly

Lay hoop over felt panel so that about ¼ of the bottom of hoop will be covered when you fold it over. Use sewing thread and needle to sew felt around hoop. Trim felt panel and sew across top.

Arrange flowers and glue in place with fabric glue on felt.

Let it dry.

Trim any excess felt as needed.

lovely Nursing Cover

With this light and airy cover, both baby and mother can have the privacy they need. The cover also doubles as a blanket for naps and quick outings.

Yarn
Premier Anti-Pilling Everyday Worsted Yarn; medium weight #4; 100% acrylic; 3.5 oz (141 g)/256 yds (234 m) per skein
- 2 skeins each: 100-23 Mist (**A**), 100-85 Azalea (**B**), 100-55 Soft Peach (**C**)

Hook and Other Materials
- US size H-8 (5 mm) crochet hook
- Yarn needle

Finished Measurements
24 in (61 cm) wide x 26 in (66 cm) long

Gauge
14 sc = 4 in (10.2 cm)
Adjust hook size if necessary to obtain gauge.

Special Stitch
2-Double Crochet Puff (2-dc puff): (Yarn over, insert hook in next st, yarn over, draw yarn through st, yarn over, draw through 2 loops on hook) 2 times in same st, yarn over, draw yarn through 3 loops on hook.

Pattern Notes
- When changing colors, complete the stitch before the color change until the last pull-through; drop working yarn, pull through next color as last pull-through to complete color change, and finish stitch. See photo tutorial on page 174.
- The beginning ch-3 counts as first dc.
- The beginning ch-4 counts as first dc plus ch 1.

INSTRUCTIONS

With A, ch 94.

Row 1 (RS): Dc in 6th ch from hook, *ch 1, sk next ch, dc in next ch; rep from across. (46 dc)

Rows 2–3: Ch 1, turn, sc in each st across. (91 sc)

Row 4: Ch 4 (counts as dc and ch 1), sk next st, *(dc, ch 1) in next st, sk next sc; rep from * across to last st, dc in last st. Fasten off.

Join B.

Row 5: Ch 3 (counts as dc), turn, dc in same st, *ch 2, sk next ch-1 sp, sc in next ch-1 sp, ch 2, sk next ch-1 sp**, (dc, ch 2, dc) in next dc; rep from * across, ending last rep at **, 2 dc in last dc.

Row 6: Ch 4, turn, 2-dc puff in first dc, ch 1, sk next 2 ch-2 sps, *(2-dc puff, ch 1, 2-dc puff, ch 1, 2-dc puff) in next ch-2 sp, ch 1, sk next 2 ch-2 sps; rep from * across to last 2 sts, sk next dc, (2 dc, ch 1, dc) in last st. Fasten off.

Join A.

Row 7: Ch 4, turn, sk next ch-1 sp, *dc in next st, ch 1, sk next ch-1 sp; rep from * across to last st, dc in last st.

Rows 8–10: Rep Rows 2–4. Fasten off.

Join C.

Rows 11–12: Rep Rows 5 and 6. Fasten off.

Join A.

Rows 13–16: Rep Row 7, followed by Rows 2–4. Fasten off.

Join B.

Rows 17–18: Rep Rows 5 and 6. Fasten off.

Join A.

Row 19: Rep Row 7.

Rows 20–58: Rep Rows 8–19, ending on Row 10.

Join A.

Row 59: Rep Row 7.

Row 60: Rep Row 2.

Fasten off. Weave in ends.

Baby Changing Mat

Keep this changing mat on hand as a quick blankie to lay baby on to change, or use it as a mat for play or feeding.

Yarn
Lion Brand Landscapes Fusion; medium weight #4; 100% acrylic; 3.5 oz (100 g)/109 yds (100 m) per skein
• 2 skeins: 544-201 Flushing Meadows

Hook and Other Materials
• US size J-10 (6 mm) crochet hook
• Yarn needle

Finished Measurements
18 in (45.7 cm) wide x 20 in (50.8 cm) long

Gauge
12 dc = 4 in (10.2 cm)
Adjust hook size if necessary to obtain gauge.

Pattern Note
The beginning ch-3 counts as first dc.

INSTRUCTIONS
Ch 73.

Row 1 (RS): Dc in 4th ch from hook, ch 1, dc in next ch, *sk next ch, dc in next ch, ch 1, dc in next ch; rep from * across to last 2 chs, sk next ch, dc in last.

Row 2: Ch 3 (counts as dc), turn, (dc, ch 1, dc) in each ch-1 sp across to last ch-1 sp, dc in 3rd ch of turning ch.

Rows 3–34 (or to desired length): Rep Row 2.
Fasten off.
Weave in ends.

Ripple Car Seat Cover

With this car seat cover, protect the baby from the sun and wind, and send the signal to let the baby sleep! The car seat cover can also be used as a blanket, so you don't have to pack an extra.

Yarn
Universal Yarns Color Burst; light weight #3, 35% acrylic and 65% superwash fine merino; 5 oz (141 g)/256 yds (234 m) per skein
• 1 skein: 106 Earth & Sky

Hook and Other Materials
• US size I-9 (5.5 mm) crochet hook
• Yarn needle
• 4 Velcro dots
• Fabric glue

Finished Measurements
28 in (71 cm) wide x 50 in (127 cm) long

Gauge
15 dc = 4 in (10.2 cm)
Adjust hook size if necessary to obtain gauge.

Get your hooks ready for this textured treat! Even though it's a simple, two-row repeat, this blanket is riddled with texture and interest. You'll have this beauty completed before you know it!

Yarn
Cascade Yarns Cherub Chunky; bulky weight #5; 55% nylon/45% acrylic; 3.5 oz (100 g)/136.7 yds (125 m) per skein
- 8 skeins: 64 Marine Blue

Hook and Other Materials
- US size K-10½ (6.5 mm) crochet hook
- Yarn needle

Finished Measurements
28 in (71 cm) wide x 50 in (127 cm) long

Gauge
12 dc = 4 in (10.2 cm)
Adjust hook size if necessary to obtain gauge.

Special Stitches
Front Post Double Crochet (FPdc): Yarn over, insert hook from front to back around post of st indicated, yarn over and pull up a loop (3 loops on hook), (yarn over and draw through 2 loops on hook) twice. See photo tutorial on page 170.

Front Post Treble Crochet (FPtr): Yarn over 2 times, insert hook from front to back to front around post of st indicated, yarn over and pull up a loop, (yarn over and draw through 2 loops on hook) 3 times. See photo tutorial on page 172.

Pattern Note
The beginning ch-3 counts as first dc.

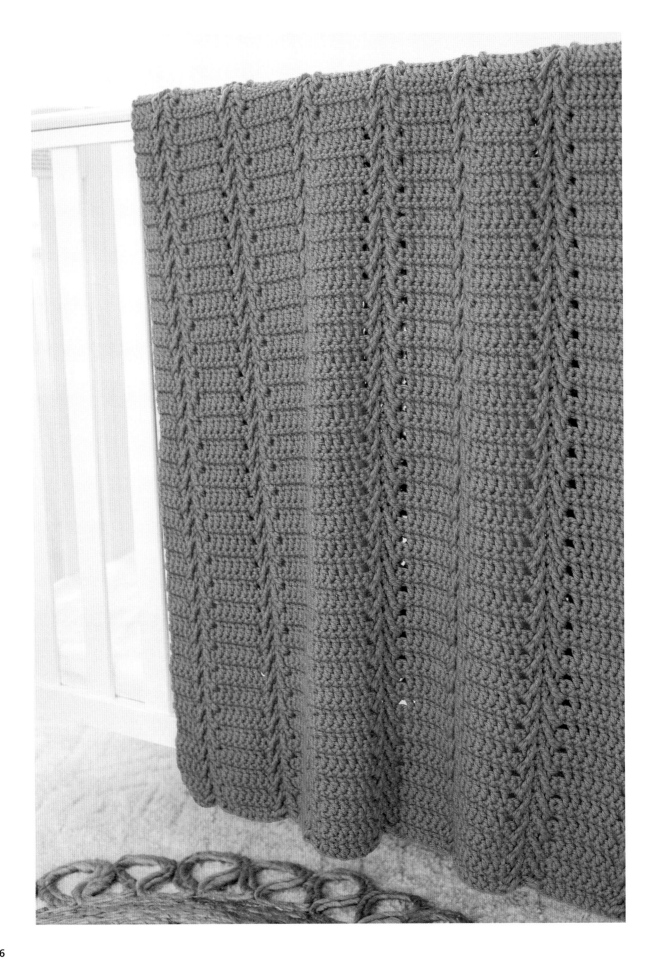

INSTRUCTIONS

Ch 88.

Row 1 (RS): Dc in 4th ch from hook and in next 2 chs, *sk next ch, dc in next 2 chs, working in front of last 2 dc made, dc in skipped ch, sk next 2 chs, dc in next, working behind last dc made, dc in each of 2 skipped chs, dc in next 6 chs; rep from * across, ending with dc in last 4 chs. (86 dc)

Row 2: Ch 1, turn, sc in each st across.

Row 3: Ch 3, turn, dc in next 3 sc, *sk next sc, dc in next 2 sc, working in front of last 2 dc made, FPtr around post of dc one row below skipped sc, sk next 2 dc in one row below, FPtr around post of dc below next sc, working behind last FPtr made, dc in each of 2 skipped sc, sk next sc, dc in next 6 sc; rep from * across ending with dc in last 4 sts.

Rows 4–116: Rep Rows 2 and 3, ending with Row 2.

Fasten off.

Weave in ends.

Hot–Air Balloon Mobile

Sweet dreams are made of adorable, tiny hot-air balloons and pom-pom clouds. This mobile adds character and playfulness without skewing totally cutesy!

Yarn

Valley Yarns Valley Superwash; medium weight #4; 100% extra fine merino; 1.75 oz (50 g)/98 yds (90 m) per skein

- 1 skein each: 301 Whisper (**A**), 522 Teal (**B**), 307 Coral (**C**), 320 Plum (**D**), 612 Grass (**E**), 300 Golden Era (**F**), 260 White (**G**)

Hook and Other Materials

- US size D-3 (3.25 mm) crochet hook
- Yarn needle
- 10-in (25.5-cm) diameter wooden hoop
- Metal ring about 1½ in (4 cm in diameter)
- Large and small pom-pom makers
- Poly-Fil stuffing

Finished Measurements

Hot-air balloon: 6 in (15.2 cm)

Gauge

16 sc = 4 in (10.2 cm)
Gauge does not have to be exact for this project.

Special Stitches

Single Crochet 2 Together (sc2tog): (Insert hook, yarn over, pull up loop) in each of the stitches indicated, yarn over, draw through all loops on hook. See photo tutorial on page 167.

Picot: Ch 3, sl st to 1st ch.

Pattern Notes

- When changing colors, complete the stitch before the color change until the last pull-through; drop working yarn, pull through next color as last pull-through to complete color change, and finish stitch. See photo tutorial on page 174.

- When working Rnds 5–25, do not carry the yarn around. Drop the yarn after completing the section after the next color change is made. When the yarn is needed in the next rnd, pick up the yarn and pull it to the next st, stranding the yarn behind the work. Do not pull tightly.
- For photo tutorial on working into back loop (BLO), see page 162.

INSTRUCTIONS

Balloon

With A, create a magic ring.

Rnd 1 (RS): 6 sc in magic ring; join with sl st to first sc. (6 sc)

Rnd 2: Ch 1, 2 sc in each st around; join with sl st to first sc. (12 sc)

Rnd 3: Ch 1, *sc in next st, 2 sc in next st; rep from * around; join with sl st to first sc. (18 sc)

Rnd 4: Ch 1, *sc in next 2 sts, 2 sc in next st; rep from * around; join with sl st to first sc. (24 sc)

Note: For Rnds 5–25, change colors after each "repeat" in the following order: B, C, D, G, E, and F.

Rnd 5: *Sc in next 3 sts, 2 sc in next st; rep from * around; do not join. (30 sc)

Rnd 6: *Sc in next 4 sts, 2 sc in next st; rep from * around. (36 sc)

Rnd 7: *Sc in next 5 sts, 2 sc in next st; rep from * around. (42 sc)

Rnd 8: *Sc in next 6 sts, 2 sc in next st; rep from * around. (48 sc)

Rnds 9–16: *Sc in next 8 sts; rep from * around.

Rnd 17: *Sc in next 3 sts, sc2tog, sc in next 3 sts; rep from * around. (42 sc)

Rnd 18: *Sc in next 3 sts, sc2tog, sc in next 2 sts; rep from * around. (36 sc)

Rnd 19: *Sc in next 6 sts; rep from * around.

Rnd 20: *Sc in next 2 sts, sc2tog, sc in next 2 sts; rep from * around. (30 sc)

Rnd 21: *Sc in next 5 sts; rep from * around.

Rnd 22: *Sc in next 2 sts, sc2tog, sc in next st; rep from * around. (24 sc)

Rnd 23: *Sc in next 4 sts; rep from * around.

Rnd 24: *Sc in next st, sc2tog, sc in next st; rep from * around. (18 sc)

Rnd 25: *Sc in next 3 sts; rep from * around; join with sl st to first sc.

Join A. Fasten off B, C, D, E, F, and G.

Rnd 26: Ch 1, sc in each st around; join with sl st to first sc. (18 sc)

Rnds 27–29: Ch 1, working in the BLO, sc in each st around; join with sl st to first sc. (18 sc)

Rnd 30: Ch 2, working in the BLO, *sc in the next st, sc2tog; rep from * around. (12 sc)

Rnd 31: Ch 1, (sc2tog) 6 times; join with sl st to first sc.

Fasten off, leaving a long tail for sewing.

Thread yarn needle with long tail and sew Rnd 31 closed.

Pom-poms

Make 3 large pom-poms each in A and G.

Make 10 small pom-poms in random colors using B–F.

Assembly

Cut six 60-in (152.5-cm) strands in G. Hold these strands together and overhand knot together to create a hanging loop. You will have six strands to attach to the hoop. At this point, the easiest way to work is to suspend the hanging loop from a hook. You could also slip the small ring over the top of a hanger, and then hang the hanger from a doorknob. Wrap strand over and around hoop, drawing out the strand so that the large ring hangs 10 in (25.5 cm) below the ring. Repeat with four strands, spacing the strands evenly around the large ring. Leave one strand in the middle. When you are happy with the position of the ring, knot in place to the ring so it will not slip out of position. Thread the end of one strand into the yarn needle. Slide one pom-pom on the strand, and then knot the end of the strand below the pom-pom. Add the large pom-pom, knot about halfway, knot below large pom-pom, and then add another small pom-pom a little lower and knot. Trim end of strand. Repeat on each strand around hoop.

To complete the middle strand: Thread the yarn needle with the middle strand. Slide one large pom-pom even with the hoop. Knot the end of the strand below the pom-pom. Next, thread the top of the balloon and adjust the height; knot the end of the strand to the top. Fasten off, leaving a long tail. Thread the tail through the hot-air balloon to weave in ends.

Banner/Garland

With B, ch 10, *picot, ch 2, dc in 2nd ch before picot, ch 10; rep from * 35 times; fasten off.

Wrap around the hoop loosely and join ends with a knot. You can adjust the banner by increasing or decreasing repeats to desired length.

Daydream Blanket

This stash-busting blanket is pure baby bliss. It's not only colorful but also the perfect size for a quick project (a.k.a. last-minute gift!).

Yarn

Knit Picks Preciosa Tonal Worsted; medium weight #4; 100% merino wool; 3.5 oz (100 g)/273 yds (250 m) per skein
- 1 skein each: 27747 Thistle (**A**), 27740 Sea Breeze (**B**), 27742 Summer Sky (**C**), 27739 Cacti (**D**), 27738 Butternut (**E**)

Hook and Other Materials

- US size J-10 (6 mm) crochet hook
- Yarn needle

Finished Measurements

26 in (66 cm) wide x 40 in (102 cm) long

Gauge

15 dc = 4 in (10.2 cm)
Adjust hook size if necessary to obtain gauge.

Special Stitch

Front Post Single Crochet (FPsc): Insert hook from front to back to front around post of st indicated, yarn over and pull up a loop, yarn over and draw through 2 loops on hook. See photo tutorial on working into stitch posts on page 170.

Pattern Notes

- When changing colors, complete the stitch before the color change until the last pull-through; drop working yarn, pull through next color as last pull-through to complete color change, and finish stitch. See photo tutorial on page 174.
- The beginning ch-2 of a round will not count as a stitch unless otherwise indicated.
- The beginning ch-3 counts as first dc.
- The beginning ch-4 counts as first dc plus ch 1 or tr; follow specific instructions per row.

INSTRUCTIONS

With A, ch 95.

Row 1 (RS): Dc in 4th ch from hook and in each ch across. (93 dc)

Row 2: Ch 4 (counts as dc and ch 1), turn, sk next st, dc in next st, *ch 1, sk next st, dc in next st; rep from * across. (47 dc, 46 ch-1 sps)

Row 3: Ch 3 (counts as first dc), turn, *dc in next ch-1 sp, dc in next dc; rep from * across. (93 dc)

Row 4: Rep Row 2.

Row 5: Rep Row 3.

Row 6: Ch 2 (not a st), turn, sk first 2 dc, dc in next dc, ch 3, 3 dc around post of last dc made, *sk next 3 dc, dc in next st, ch 3, 3 dc around post of last dc made; rep from * across to last 2 sts, sk 1 st, dc in last st. (23 groups)

Row 7: Ch 4 (counts as tr), turn, *sk next 4 dc, dc in top of next ch-3 loop, ch 3, 3 dc around post of last dc made; rep from * across to turning ch, tr in 2nd ch of turning ch. (23 groups, 2 tr)

Row 8: Ch 4 (counts as dc and ch 1), turn, *sk next 4 dc, sc in top of next ch 3 loop**, ch 3; rep from * across ending last rep at **, ch 1, dc in last st.

Row 9: Ch 3 (counts as dc), turn, dc in next ch-1 sp, *dc in next sc, 3 dc in next ch-3 loop; rep from * across to last ch-3 loop, dc in next sc, dc in ch-1 sp, dc in last st.

Row 10: Rep Row 2.

Row 11: Rep Row 3.

Row 12: Rep Row 4.

Row 13: Rep Row 5.

Row 14: Ch 1, FPsc in each st across. Fasten off.

Join B.

Row 15: Ch 3 (counts as dc), dc in each st across.

Rows 16–28: Rep Rows 2–14. Fasten off.

Join C.

Row 29: Rep Row 15.

Rows 30–42: Rep Rows 2–14. Fasten off.

Join D.

Row 43: Rep Row 15.

Rows 44–56: Rep Rows 2–14. Fasten off.

Join E.

Row 57: Rep Row 15.

Rows 58–70: Rep Rows 2–14. Fasten off.

Weave in ends.

Ultimate
Storage Basket

Never underestimate storage in a nursery. Baskets and bins are a good option and can be repurposed as the child grows. This one can store all the toys or burp cloths, and it looks fun too!

Yarn

Lion Brand Basic Stitch; medium weight #4; 100% acrylic; 3.5 oz (100 g)/185 yds (170 m) per skein
- 6 skeins: 202-100 White (**A**)
- 1 skein each: 202-142 Prism (**B**), 202-105 Frost (**C**)

Lion Brand Basic Stitch Premium; medium weight #4; 100% acrylic; 3.5 oz (100 g)/219 yds (200 m) per skein
- 1 skein: 201-158 Saffron (**D**)

Hook and Other Materials
- US size K-10½ (6.5 mm) crochet hook
- Yarn needle
- Small pom-pom maker
- Stitch markers

Finished Measurements

15 in (38 cm) base diameter x 13 in (33 cm) high

Gauge

With 2 strands held together: 12 sc = 4 in (10.2 cm)
Adjust hook size if necessary to obtain gauge.

Special Stitch

Single Crochet 2 Together (sc2tog): (Insert hook, yarn over, pull up loop) in each of the stitches indicated, yarn over, draw through all loops on hook. See photo tutorial on page 167.

Pattern Notes

- When changing colors, complete the stitch before the color change until the last pull-through; drop working yarn, pull through next color as last pull-through to complete color change, and finish stitch. See photo tutorial on page 174.
- Hold 2 strands of indicated colors together throughout.
- For photo tutorial on working into the back loop (BLO), see page 162.

INSTRUCTIONS

Rnd 1 (RS): With 2 strands of A held together, create magic ring, 10 sc in ring; do not join. (10 sc) Place marker to indicate beginning of rnd.

Note: Loop a short piece of yarn around any stitch to mark Rnd 1 as RS.

Rnd 2: 2 sc in each st around. (20 sc)

Rnd 3: *Sc in next st, 2 sc in next st; rep from * around. (30 sc)

Rnd 4: *Sc in next 2 sts, 2 sc in next st; rep from * around. (40 sc)

Rnd 5: *Sc in next 3 sts, 2 sc in next st; rep from * around. (50 sc)

Rnd 6: *Sc in next 4 sts, 2 sc in next st; rep from * around. (60 sc)

Rnd 7: *Sc in next 5 sts, 2 sc in next st; rep from * around. (70 sc)

Rnd 8: *Sc in next 6 sts, 2 sc in next st; rep from * around. (80 sc)

Rnd 9: *Sc in next 7 sts, 2 sc in next st; rep from * around. (90 sc)

Rnd 10: *Sc in next 8 sts, 2 sc in next st; rep from * around. (100 sc)

Rnd 11: *Sc in next 9 sts, 2 sc in next st; rep from * around. (110 sc)

Rnd 12: *Sc in next 10 sts, 2 sc in next st; rep from * around. (120 sc)

Rnd 13: *Sc in next 11 sts, 2 sc in next st; rep from * around. (130 sc)

Rnd 14: *Sc in next 12 sts, 2 sc in next st; rep from * around. (140 sc)

Rnd 15: *Sc in next 13 sts, 2 sc in next st; rep from * around. (150 sc)

Rnds 16–17: Sc in each st around.

Rnd 18: Working in the BLO, sc in each st around.

Rnds 19–45: Sc in each st around.

Rnd 46: *Sc in next 13 sts, sc2tog; rep from * around. (140 sc)

Rnds 47–48: Sc in each st around.

Rnd 49: *Sc in next 12 sts, sc2tog; rep from * around. (130 sc)

Rnds 50–51: Sc in each st around.

Rnd 52: *Sc in next 11 sts, sc2tog; rep from * around. (120 sc)

Fasten off one strand of A; join 1 strand of C.

Rnd 53: *Sc in next 8 sts, sc2tog; rep from * around; join with sl st to first sc. (108 sc)

Rnd 54: Sc in each st around; join with sl st to first sc.

Rnd 55: *Sc in next 7 sts, sc2tog; rep from * around; join with sl st to first sc. (96 sc)

Do not fasten off A. Fasten off C; join D.

Rnd 56: Sc in each st around; join with sl st to first sc.

Rnd 57: *Sc in next 6 sts, sc2tog; rep from * around; join with sl st to first sc. (84 sc)

Rnd 58: Sc in each st around; join with sl st to first sc.

Do not fasten off A. Fasten off D; join B.

Rnds 59–60: Sc in each st around; join with sl st to first sc. Fasten off.

Weave in ends.

Pom-poms

Make 10 small pom-poms each in B, C, and D according to pom-pom maker package instructions.

Tie pom-poms on outside of basket in a random order.

Carter Basket

Looking for a quick catchall or diaper storage for the changing table? Not only is this basket the perfect size, but it has a fun charted design too.

Yarn

Valley Yarns Valley Superwash; medium weight #4; 100% extra fine merino; 1.75 oz (50 g)/98 yds (90 m) per skein

- 1 skein each: 301 Whisper (**A**), 303 Daiquiri Ice (**B**), 300 Golden Era (**C**)

Hook and Other Materials

- US size 7 (4.5 mm) crochet hook
- Yarn needle

Finished Measurements

7½ in (19 cm) long x 5½ in (14 cm) wide x 4¼ in (11 cm) high

Gauge

16 sc x 19 rows = 4 in (10.2 cm)
Adjust hook size if necessary to obtain gauge.

Special Stitches

Single Crochet 2 Together (sc2tog): (Insert hook, yarn over, pull up loop) in each of the stitches indicated, yarn over, draw through all loops on hook. See photo tutorial on page 167.

Waistcoat Stitch (WC): Insert hook between the "legs" of the next st, yarn over and draw up a loop, yarn over and draw through both loops on hook. The waistcoat stitch is worked like a single crochet *except* that the hook is inserted between the two leaning vertical strands that form a V on the front of the st, instead of under the top 2 loops.

Reverse Single Crochet (rev sc): Single crochet worked from left to right (right to left, if left-handed). Insert hook into next stitch to the right (left), under loop on hook, and draw up a loop. Yarn over, draw through all loops on hook. See photo tutorial on page 173.

Pattern Notes

- When changing colors, complete the stitch before the color change until the last pull-through; drop working yarn, pull through next color as last pull-through to complete color change, and finish stitch. See photo tutorial on page 174.
- Basket is made in 2 sections: base and body.
- Each square of chart represents one Waistcoat Stitch (WC). Read each rnd of chart from right to left.
- For photo tutorial on working into the back loop (BLO), see page 162.

INSTRUCTIONS

Base
With A, ch 31.

Row 1 (RS): Sc in 2nd ch from hook and in each ch across. (30 sc)

Rows 2–25: Ch 1, turn, sc in each st across. Do not fasten off.

Body
Rnd 1 (RS): Ch 1, turn, sc in next 30 sts, sc 25 evenly across end of rows, sc 30 across Row 1, sc evenly across end of rows; join with sl st to first sc. (110 sc)

Rnd 2: Ch 1, working in the BLO, sc in each st around; join with sl st to first sc.

Rnds 3–4: WC in each st around; do not join.

Rnds 5–15: Begin with Rnd 1 of chart, use WC stitch, work rnds and change yarn color following chart until all 11 rnds of chart have been completed.

Rnds 16–22: With A, WC in each st around.

Rnd 23: *Sc in next 8 sts, sc2tog; rep from * around; join with sl st to first sc. Fasten off A.

Rnd 24: Join C, ch 1, rev sc in each st around; join with sl st to first sc.

Fasten off.

Weave in ends.

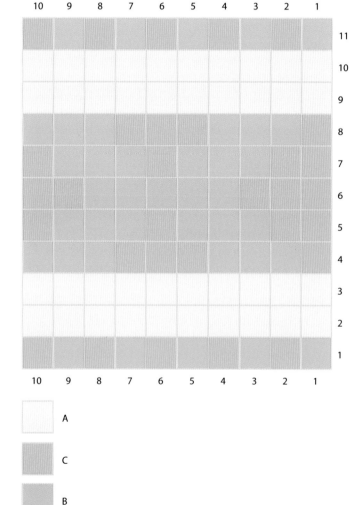

Bear lovey

Playtime! Naptime! Travel time! Lovey time! Okay, you get it. This is a must-have for the baby. It's the perfect size to carry around and give comfort during any event of the day.

Yarn

Red Heart Soft; medium weight #4; 100% acrylic; 5 oz (141 g)/256 yds (234 m) per skein
- 1 skein each: Mercury (**A**), Cosmos (**B**)

Hook and Other Materials
- US size J-10 (6 mm) crochet hook
- Yarn needle
- Poly-Fil stuffing
- Small pom-pom maker
- Scrap of black yarn for face
- Stitch markers

Finished Measurements

Lovey: 11 in x 11 in (28 cm x 28 cm)

Gauge

14 sc x 16 rows = 4 in (10.2 cm)
Adjust hook size if necessary to obtain gauge.

Special Stitches

Back Post Single Crochet (BPsc): Insert hook from back to front to back around post of st indicated, yarn over and pull up a loop, yarn over and draw through 2 loops on hook.

Front Post Single Crochet (FPsc): Insert hook from front to back to front around post of st indicated, yarn over and pull up a loop, yarn over and draw through 2 loops on hook.

Single Crochet 2 Together (sc2tog): (Insert hook, yarn over, pull up loop) in each of the stitches indicated, yarn over, draw through all loops on hook. See photo tutorial on page 167.

Pattern Notes
- When changing colors, complete the stitch before the color change until the last pull-through; drop working yarn, pull through next color as last pull-through to complete color change, and finish stitch. See photo tutorial on page 174.
- The beginning ch-3 counts as first dc.
- See photo tutorial for working into stitch posts on page 170.

INSTRUCTIONS

Lovey

With A, ch 4; join with sl st in first ch to form a ring.

Rnd 1 (RS): Ch 3 (counts as dc in this rnd and in all following rnds), 2 dc in ring, ch 2, (3 dc in ring, ch 2) 3 times; join with sl st in top of beg ch. (12 dc and 4 ch-2 sps)

Rnd 2: Sl st next 2 dc, (sl st, ch 3, 2 dc, ch 2, 3 dc) in first ch-2 sp (beg corner made), ch 1, *(3 dc, ch 2, 3 dc) in next ch-2 sp (corner made), ch 1; rep from * around; join with sl st in top of beg ch. (24 dc, 4 ch-2 sps and 4 ch-1 sps)

Bear Head

With A, ch 2.

Rnd 1 (RS): 6 sc in 2nd ch from hook and in each ch across; do not join. (6 sc) Place marker to indicate beginning of rnd.

Note: Loop a short piece of yarn around any stitch to mark Rnd 1 as RS.

Rnd 2: 2 sc in each st around. (12 sc)

Rnd 3: *Sc in next st, 2 sc in next st; rep from * around. (18 sc)

Rnd 4: *Sc in next 2 sts, 2 sc in next st; rep from * around. (24 sc)

Rnd 5: *Sc in next 3 sts, 2 sc in next st; rep from * around. (30 sc)

Rnd 6: *Sc in next 4 sts, 2 sc in next st; rep from *around. (36 sc)

Rnds 7–10: Sc in each st around. (36 sc)

Rnd 11: *Sc in next 4 sts; sc2tog; rep from * around. (30 sc)

Rnd 12: *Sc in next 3 sts; sc2tog; rep from * around. (24 sc)

Rnd 13: *Sc in next 2 sts; sc2tog; rep from * around. (18 sc)

Rnd 3: Sl st in next 2 dc, (sl st, ch 3, 2 dc, ch 2, 3 dc) in first ch-2 sp, ch 1, 3 dc in next ch-1 sp, ch 1, *(3 dc, ch 2, 3 dc) in next corner ch-2 sp, ch 1, 3 dc in next ch-1 sp, ch 1; rep from * around; join with sl st in top of beg ch. (36 dc, 4 ch-2 sps and 8 ch-1 sps)

Rnd 4: Sl st in next 2 dc, (sl st, ch 3, 2 dc, ch 2, 3 dc) in first ch-2 sp, ch 1, (3 dc in next ch-1 sp, ch 1) to next corner, *(3 dc, ch 2, 3 dc) in corner ch-2 sp, ch 1, (3 dc in next ch-1 sp, ch 1) to next corner; rep from * around; join with sl st in top of beg ch. Fasten off.

Rnds 5–8: Rep Rnd 4. Fasten off.

Rnd 9: With RS facing, join B with sl st in any ch-2 sp, ch 3, (2 dc, ch 2, 3 dc) in same ch-2 sp, ch 1, (3 dc in next ch-1 sp, ch 1) to next corner, *(3 dc, ch 2, 3 dc) in corner ch-2 sp, ch 1, (3 dc in next ch-1 sp, ch 1) to next corner; rep from * around; join with sl st in top of beg ch. Fasten off B.

Rnd 10: With RS facing, join A in any ch-1 sp, ch 1, 3 sc in same sp, sc in each st and ch-1 sp around with 3 sc in each ch-2 sp; join with sl st to first sc. Fasten off.

Rnd 14: *Sc in next st; sc2tog; rep from * around. (12 sc)

Rnd 15: (Sc2tog) 6 times; join with a sl st to first sc. Fasten off, leaving a long tail.

Thread yarn needle with tail and close Rnd 15.

Ear (make 2)

With A, ch 2.

Rnd 1: 4 sc in 2nd ch from hook; do not join. (4 sc) Place marker to indicate beginning of rnd.

Note: Loop a short piece of yarn around any stitch to mark Rnd 1 as RS.

Rnd 2: 2 sc in each st around. (8 sc)

Rnd 3: *Sc in next st; 2 sc in next st; rep from * around. (12 sc)

Rnd 4: (Sc2tog) 6 times. (6 sc)

Fasten off, leaving a long tail for sewing.

Hat

With B, ch 2.

Rnd 1 (RS): 6 sc in 2nd ch from hook and in each ch across; do not join. (6 sc) Place marker to indicate beginning of rnd.

Note: Loop a short piece of yarn around any stitch to mark Rnd 1 as RS.

Rnd 2: 2 sc in each st around. (12 sc)

Rnd 3: *Sc in next st, 2 sc in next st; rep from * around. (18 sc)

Rnd 4: *Sc in next 2 sts, 2 sc in next st; rep from * around. (24 sc)

Rnd 5: *Sc in next 3 sts, 2 sc in next st; rep from * around. (30 sc)

Rnd 6: *Sc in next 4 sts, 2 sc in next st; rep from * around. (36 sc)

Rnds 7–9: Sc in each st around.

Rnds 10–11: *BPsc on next st, FPsc on next st; rep from * around.

Fasten off, leaving a long tail for sewing.

Assembly and Finishing

Use yarn needle and sew hat on head.

Sew ears on hat.

Make 1 pom-pom according to pom-pom maker package directions.

Attach pom-pom to top of hat.

Thread scrap black yarn in yarn needle and, using photo as a guide, stitch on face.

Use yarn needle and sew center of lovey onto bottom of head.

Handy Wipes Case

I'm sure you love how cute and fashionable plastic wipes bags are as much as I do—not! But this one has a pretty pattern and colors. This is the perfect mini bag to have on hand "just in case." Throw it in the wash and use it again and again!

Yarn

Red Heart Soft; medium weight #4; 100% acrylic; 5 oz (141 g)/256 yds (234 m) per skein
- 1 skein: Treasure Island

Hooks and Other Materials

- US size 7 (4.5 mm) crochet hook
- Yarn needle
- Stitch marker
- 2 Velcro dots
- Fabric glue

Finished Measurements

8 in x 6 in (20 cm x 15.2 cm)

Gauge

14 sc x 16 rows = 4 in (10.2 cm)
Adjust hook size if necessary to obtain gauge.

Special Stitches

Hdc2tog: (Yarn over, insert hook in next stitch, yarn over and pull up a loop) twice, yarn over and pull through all loops on hook.

Long Sc2tog: Insert hook in st indicated in pattern, yarn over and pull up a long loop, stretching it to the height of current round (2 loops on hook); working over the next st, insert hook into next st 2 rounds below, yarn over and pull up another long loop, stretching it to the height of current round (3 loops on hook). Yarn over and pull through all 3 loops (first sc2tog made).

Pattern Note

- The wipes case is worked in the round.
- For instructions on how to work into the hdc 3rd loop, see photo tutorial on page 164.
- For photo tutorial on working into the back loop (BLO), see page 162.

INSTRUCTIONS

Ch 86; join with sl st to first ch, do not twist chain.

Rnd 1 (RS): Ch 1, sc in each ch around; join with sl st to first ch. Place marker to indicate beginning of rnd. (86)

Rnd 2: Ch 1, sc in each st around, do not join.

Rnd 3: Insert hook back into the first st one round below. *Long sc2tog, sk unworked st behind long sc2tog just made, sc in next 2 sts; rep from * around to last st, work one Long sc2tog using the last st and the first st of next rnd.

Rnds 4–22: Sc in next 2 sts, *Long sc2tog, sc in next 2 sts; rep from * around to last st; using the last and and the first st of next rnd Long sc2tog.

Fasten off, leaving a long tail for sewing.

Thread yarn needle and with WS facing, fold in half and sew one end together.

Tab

Locate the center st on one long side.

Row 1 (RS): Join yarn in 5th st to the right from center, ch 2 (not a st), hdc in next 10 sts. (10 hdc)

Row 2: Ch 2, turn, hdc in first st, hdc in 3rd loop in next 8 sts, hdc in last st.

Row 3: Ch 2, working in the BLO, hdc in each st across.

Rows 4–17: Rep Row 2 and Row 3.

Row 18: Rep Row 2.

Row 19: Ch 2, working in the BLO, hdc2tog, hdc in next 6 sts, hdc2tog. Fasten off.

Weave in ends.

Finishing

Glue a Velcro dot to WS of tab.

Glue a Velcro dot to outside of case to match placement of tab.

Woodland loafers

Little loafers are not only for keeping feet warm—placed strategically on a shelf, they can act as decor! Plus, when you make something this cute, you have to show it off!

Yarn

Lion Brand Vanna's Choice; medium weight #4; 100% acrylic; 3.5 oz (100 grams)/170 yds (156 m) per skein

- 1 skein each: 860-130 Honey (**A**), 860-098 Fisherman (**B**), 860-125 Taupe (**C**)

Hook and Other Materials

- US size F-5 (3.75 mm) crochet hook
- Yarn needle
- Stitch markers

Sizes/Finished Measurements

Small: 2 in (5 cm) wide x 3 in (7.5 cm) long
Medium: 2 in (5 cm) wide x 3½ in (9 cm) long
Large: 2¼ in (5.5 cm) wide x 3½ in (9 cm) long

Gauge

8 sc and 9 rows = 2 in (5 cm)
Adjust hook size if necessary to obtain gauge.

Special Stitches

Double Crochet 2 Together (dc2tog): Yarn over, pull up a loop in next stitch, yarn over, pull through first 2 loops, yarn over, pull up a loop in the next stitch, yarn over and draw through first 2 loops, yarn over and pull through all loops on hook (counts as 1 dc). See photo tutorial on page 168.

Single Crochet 2 Together (sc2tog): Pull up a loop in next 2 sts, yarn over and draw through 3 loops on hook (counts as one sc). See photo tutorial on page 167.

Pattern Notes

- For photo tutorial on working into back loop (BLO), see page 162.
- Use puffy paint on bottom of complete shoe sole as decoration.

INSTRUCTIONS

Loafer (make 2)
Sole (make 2 for each boot: 1 in A and 1 in B per boot)
Ch 10 (12, 14).

Rnd 1 (RS): Sc in second ch from hook and in next 4 (5, 6) ch, hdc in next 3 (4, 5) chs, 4 hdc in last ch; working in free loops of beginning ch, hdc in next 3 (4, 5) chs, sc in next 4 (5, 6) chs, 3 sc in next ch; join with slip st to first sc. [22 (26, 30) sts]

Note: Loop a short piece of yarn around any stitch to mark Rnd 1 as RS.

Rnd 2: Ch 1, sc in same st as joining and in next 4 (5, 6) sts, hdc in next 1 (1, 2) sts, dc in next 2 (3, 3) sts, 2 dc in next st, 2 hdc in next 2 sts, 2 dc in next st, dc in next 2 (3, 3) sts, hdc in next 1, (1, 2) sts, sc in next 4 (5, 6) sts, 2 sc in next 3 sts; join with slip st to first sc. [29 (33, 37) sts]

Rnd 3: Ch 1, hdc in same st as joining *(place marker in this st to use later)* and in next 7 (9, 11), (hdc in next st, 2 hdc in next st) 4 times, hdc in next 7 (9, 11) sts, (sc in next st, 2 sc in next st) 3 times; join with slip st to first hdc. [36 (40, 44) sts]

Large size only:

Rnd 4: Ch 1, sc in same st as joining and in next 11, (hdc in next 2 sts, 2 hdc in next st) 4 times, sc in next 11 sts, (sc in next 2 sts, 2 sc in next st) 3 times; join with slip st to first sc. (51 sts)

Joining: Hold two soles with WS together, matching sts, and marked sole on bottom. Do not begin with slipknot on hook. Holding sole in color A to the back and working through both loops of both pieces, insert hook in any st on Rnd 3 (3, 4), yarn over and pull up a loop, slip st in each st around; cut yarn. Remove hook from loop. Insert hook from back to front through center of first st, hook loop and draw through, yarn over and pull end through loop.

Sides and Toe
Rnd 1 (RS): With sole in color A away from you and working in the BLO, join C with sc in marked st; remove marker, sc in each st around; join with slip st to first sc. [36 (40, 44) sc]

Rnd 2: Ch 2, sc in both loops of each sc around; join with slip st to first sc.

Rnd 3: Ch 1, sc in same st as joining and in next 13 (15, 17) sc, working in BLO, dc2tog 8 times, sc in both loops of last 6 (8, 10) sc; join with slip st to first sc. [28 (32, 36) sts]

Rnd 4: Ch 1, sc in same st as joining and in next 13 (15, 17) sc, dc2tog 4 times, sc in last 6 (8, 10) sc; join with slip st to first sc. [24 (28, 32) sts]

Rnd 5: Ch 1, sc in same st as joining and in next 13 (15, 17) sc, dc2tog twice, sc in last 6 (8, 10) sc; join with slip st to first sc. [22 (26, 30) sts]

Rnd 6: Ch 1, sc in same st as joining, hdc in next st, dc in next 6 (8, 10) sts, hdc in next st, sc in last 13 (15, 17) sts; join with slip st to first sc. [22 (26, 30) sts]

Rnd 7: Ch 1, sc in each st around; join with slip st to first sc. Fasten off.

Tab
Using A, ch 11.

Row 1 (RS): Sc in back ridge of second ch from hook and each ch across. (10 sc)

Row 2: Ch 1, turn; sc in each sc across. Fasten off.

Use yarn needle to sew tab onto back of loafer.

Relaxing Footstool (Pouf)

Fashion meets function with this oversized pouf. Mom can kick up her feet and enjoy snuggling the baby in comfort!

Yarn

Red Heart Hygge; medium weight #4; 100% acrylic; 8 oz (227 g)/212 yds (194 m) per skein
- 2 skeins each: E881-8369 Latte (**A**), E881-8319 Rust (**B**)

Hook and Other Materials

- US size J-10 (6 mm) crochet hook
- Yarn needle
- 2 standard pillows
- Stitch markers

Finished Measurements

28 in (71 cm) wide x 48 in (122 cm) long

Gauge

14 dc = 4 in (10.2 cm)
Adjust hook size if necessary to obtain gauge.

Special Stitch

Double Crochet 2 Together (dc2tog): Yarn over, pull up a loop in next stitch, yarn over, pull through first 2 loops, yarn over, pull up a loop in the next stitch, yarn over and draw through first 2 loops, yarn over and pull through all loops on hook (counts as 1 dc). See photo tutorial on page 168.

Pattern Notes

- The beginning ch-2 of a round will not count as a stitch unless otherwise indicated.
- When changing colors, complete the stitch before the color change until the last pull-through; drop working yarn, pull through next color as last pull-through to complete color change, and finish stitch. See photo tutorial on page 174.

INSTRUCTIONS

Rnd 1 (RS): With A, create a magic ring, 12 dc in ring; do not join. (12 dc) Place marker to indicate beginning of rnd.

Note: Loop a short piece of yarn around any stitch to mark Rnd 1 as RS.

Rnd 2: Ch 2 (not a st here and throughout), 2 dc in each st around; join with sl st to first dc. (24 dc)

Rnd 3: Ch 2, *dc in next st, 2 dc in next st; rep from * around; join with sl st to first dc. (36 dc)

Rnd 4: Ch 2, *dc in next 2 sts, 2 dc in next st; rep from * around; join with sl st to first dc. (48 dc)

Rnd 5: Ch 2, *dc in next 3 sts, 2 dc in next st; rep from * around; join with sl st to first dc. (60 dc)

Rnd 6: Ch 2, *dc in next 4 sts, 2 dc in next st; rep from * around; join with sl st to first dc. (72 dc)

Rnd 7: Ch 2, *dc in next 5 sts, 2 dc in next st; rep from * around; join with sl st to first dc. (84 dc)

Rnd 8: Ch 2, *dc in next 6 sts, 2 dc in next st; rep from * around; join with sl st to first dc. (96 dc)

Rnd 9: Ch 2, *dc in next 7 sts, 2 dc in next st; rep from * around; join with sl st to first dc. (108 dc)

Rnds 10–13: Ch 2, dc in each st around; join with sl st to first dc.

Drop A; join B.

Rnd 14: Ch 1, sc in each st around; join with sl st to first sc.

Drop B; pick up A.

Rnds 15–16: Ch 2, dc in each st around; join with sl st to first dc.

Drop A; pick up B.

Rnd 17: Ch 2, dc in each st around; join with sl st to first dc.

Drop B; pick up A.

Rnds 18–19: Ch 2, dc in each st around; join with sl st to first dc.

Drop A; pick up B.

Rnd 20: Ch 2, dc in each st around; join with sl st to first dc.

Drop B; pick up A.

Rnd 21: Ch 1, sc in each st around; join with sl st to first sc.

Drop A; pick up B.

Rnd 22: Ch 2, dc in each st around; join with sl st to first dc.

Drop B; pick up A.

Rnds 23–24: Ch 2, dc in each st around; join with sl st to first dc.

Drop A; pick up B.

Rnd 25: Ch 2, dc in each st around; join with sl st to first dc.

Drop B; pick up A.

Rnds 26–27: Ch 2, dc in each st around; join with sl st to first dc.

Drop A; pick up B.

Rnd 28: Ch 1, sc in each st around; join with sl st to first sc.

Fasten off B; pick up A.

Rnds 29–32: Ch 2, dc in each st around; join with sl st to first dc.

Rnd 33: *Dc in next 7 sts, dc2tog; rep from * around; join with sl st to first dc. (96 dc)

Rnd 34: *Dc in next 6 sts, dc2tog; rep from * around; join with sl st to first dc. (84 dc)

Rnd 35: *Dc in next 5 sts, dc2tog; rep from * around; join with sl st to first dc. (72 dc)

Rnd 36: *Dc in next 4 sts, dc2tog; rep from * around; join with sl st to first dc. (60 dc)

Cut open one pillow and remove half of the stuffing. Fold full pillow in half and place the half pillow in the middle; insert pillows into pouf.

Rnd 37: *Dc in next 3 sts, dc2tog; join with sl st to first dc. (48 dc)

Rnd 38: *Dc in next 2 sts, dc2tog; join with sl st to first dc. (36 dc)

Rnd 39: *Dc in next st, dc2tog; join with sl st to first dc. (24 dc)

Rnd 40: (Dc2tog) 12 times; join with sl st to first dc. (12 dc)

Fasten off, leaving a long tail for sewing.

Thread yarn needle with long tail and sew Rnd 40 closed.

On-the-Go
Backpack

Carry all the sweet notions in this mini backpack. The flap will keep everything in place, and the straps give you a hands-free option!

Yarn

Lion Brand Wool Ease Thick and Quick; super bulky weight #6; 80% acrylic/20% wool; 6 oz (170 g)/106 yds (97 m) per skein
- 1 skein each: 640-112 Raspberry (**A**), 640-158 Mustard (**B**)

Hook and Other Materials

- US size K-10½ (6.5 mm) crochet hook
- Yarn needle

Finished Measurements

8½ in (21.5 cm) wide x 8½ in (21.5 cm) high

Gauge

9 sc = 4 in (10.2 cm)
Adjust hook size if necessary to obtain gauge.

Special Stitch

Single Crochet 2 Together (sc2tog): (Insert hook, yarn over, pull up loop) in each of the stitches indicated, yarn over, draw through all loops on hook. See photo tutorial on page 167.

Pattern Notes

- When changing colors, complete the stitch before the color change until the last pull-through; drop working yarn, pull through next color as last pull-through to complete color change, and finish stitch. See photo tutorial on page 174.
- The beginning ch-3 counts as first dc.
- For photo tutorial on working into the back loop (BLO), see page 162.

INSTRUCTIONS

Main Body

With A, ch 4.

Rnd 1 (RS): 10 dc in 4th ch from hook; join with sl st to first dc. (10 dc)

Rnd 2: Ch 3 (counts as first dc), dc in same st as joining, 2 dc in each st around; join with sl st to beg ch-3. (20 dc)

Rnd 3: Ch 3, 2 dc in next st, *dc in next st, 2 dc in next st; rep from * around; join with sl st to beg ch-3. (30 dc)

Rnd 4: Ch 3, dc in next st, 2 dc in next st, *dc in next 2 sts, 2 dc in next st; rep from * around; join with sl st to beg ch-3. (40 dc)

Rnd 5: Ch 3, dc in next 2 sts, 2 dc in next st, *dc in next 3 sts, 2 dc in next st; rep from * around; join with sl st to beg ch-3. (50 dc)

Rnd 6: Ch 3, dc in next 3 sts, 2 dc in next st, *dc in next 4 sts, 2 dc in next st; rep from * around; join with sl st to beg ch-3. (60 dc)

Rnd 7: Ch 1, working in the BLO, sc in each st around; join with sl st to first sc.

Rnd 8: Ch 1, *sc in the BLO of next st, sc in both loops of next st; rep from * around; do not join.

Rnd 9: *Sc in both loops of next st, sc in BLO of next st; rep from * around.

Rnd 10: *Sc in BLO of next st, sc in both loops of next st; rep from * around.

Rnds 11–26: Rep Rnds 9 and 10.

Fasten off A; join B.

Rnd 27: Ch 1, sc in each st around; join with sl st to first sc. Do not fasten off.

Flap

Row 1: Ch 1, working in the BLO, sc in next 30 sts. (30 sc)

Rows 2–5: Ch 1, turn, working in the BLO, sc in each st across.

Row 6: Ch 1, turn, sc2tog, sc in each st across to last 2 sts, sc2tog. (28 sc)

Rows 7–13: Rep Row 6; decreasing by 2 sts each row, ending with 12 sc.

Row 14: (*Note: Buttonhole made on this row.*) Ch 1, sc2tog, sc in next 3 sts, ch 2, sk 2 sts, sc in next 3 sts, sc2tog. (10 sc)

Row 15: Ch 2, sc in next 4 sts, 2 sc in next ch-2 sp, sc in next 4 sts. (10 sc)

Trim

Rnd 1: Ch 1, working down edge of flap, sc evenly across ends of rows, sc in each st around front of backpack, working on opposite edge of flap, sc evenly across ends of rows, 2 sc in first st of Row 15, sc in next 8 sts, 2 sc in last st; join with sl st to first sc. Fasten off.

Top Carry Strap

With B, ch 16.

Row 1 (RS): Dc in 4th ch from hook and in each ch across. (14 dc)

Fasten off, leaving a long tail for sewing.

Backpack Straps (make 2)

With A, ch 37.

Row 1 (RS): Dc in 4th ch from hook and in each ch across. (35 dc)

Fasten off, leaving a long tail for sewing.

Finishing

Sew top carry strap on back center of flap.

Sew the top of the backpack straps on back center under the top carry strap. Sew the bottoms of the backpack straps 6 sts apart on Row 7 above the exposed front loops.

Lay flap over bag and line up button with the buttonhole. Sew button in place securely.

Weave in ends.

Curtain Tie

Help the day begin for your little sunshine with this curtain tie. It's quick and simple and an awesome stash-buster!

Yarn
Valley Yarns Valley Superwash; medium weight #4; 100% extra fine merino; 1.75 oz (50 g)/98 yds (90 m) per skein
- 1 skein: 301 Whisper

Hooks and Other Materials
- US size H-8 (5 mm) crochet hook
- Yarn needle

Finished Measurements
13 in (33 cm) wide x 4½ in (11.5 cm) long

Gauge
16 sc = 4 in (10.2 cm)
Adjust hook size if necessary to obtain gauge.

Pattern Note
The beginning ch-4 counts as the first tr.

INSTRUCTIONS
Ch 69.
Row 1 (RS): (2 dc, ch 2, 2 dc) in 6th ch from hook, *sk next 5 ch, (2 dc, ch 2, 2 dc) in next ch; rep from * across to last 3 ch, sk next 2 ch, dc in last ch.
Row 2: Ch 1, turn, sc in first dc, *ch 3, dc in next ch-2 sp, ch 3, sk next 2 dc, sc between last skipped and next dc; rep from * across, ending with sc in last sc in top of turning ch.
Row 3: Ch 4 (counts as tr), turn, sk next ch-3 loop, (2 dc, ch 2, 2 dc) in next dc, *sk next 2 ch-3 loops, (2 dc, ch 2, 2 dc) in next dc; rep from * across to last ch-3 loop, sk next ch-3 loop, tr in last sc.
Rows 4–9: Rep Rows 2 and 3. Fasten off.

Ties
Cut twelve 40 in (101 cm) lengths. Attach three strands like fringe on each corner.
On each side: Overhand knot the two corners together 2 in (5 cm) from fringe knot. Braid for 5 in (13 cm). Overhand knot and trim ends to 1½ in (4 cm).

HOW TO READ
THE PATTERNS

Symbols and Terms

* : Work instructions following * as many more times as indicated in addition to the first time.

( ) : Work enclosed instructions as many times as specified by the number immediately following or work all enclosed instructions in the stitch or space indicated or contains explanatory remarks.

( ) or [ ] at end of row or rnd: The number of stitches or spaces you should have after completing that row or round.

Gauge: Exact gauge is essential for proper size. Before beginning your project, make the sample swatch given in the individual instructions in the yarn and hook specified. After completing the swatch, measure it, counting your stitches and rows carefully. If your swatch is larger or smaller than specified, make another, changing hook size to get the correct gauge. Keep trying until you find the size hook that will give you the specified gauge.

Skill Levels:

Easy: Projects with basic stitches, repetitive stitch patterns, simple color changes, and simple shaping and finishing.

Intermediate: Projects using a variety of techniques, such as basic lace patterns or color patterns, mid-level shaping, and finishing.

Materials: Items you will need to complete the patterns in this book include crochet hooks, stitch markers, pins, scissors, yarn, ruler, a yarn needle, and other items as given in the list for each pattern.

- **Crochet hooks:** Each pattern will list the crochet hook needed for that project. Always start with the hook size stated and check the gauge before starting the project. Change the hook size as necessary to obtain the correct gauge so that the project will be finished in the correct size.
- **Stitch markers:** Stitch markers are used to mark specific stitches in a pattern. If you do not have access to ready-made markers, use a piece of scrap yarn or even a bobby pin to mark the stitch.
- **Yarn needle:** The yarn needle is a large needle with a big eye suitable for yarn, used to sew different pieces together and for weaving in ends.

Yarn: You will find listed for each pattern the specific yarn(s) and colors I used to crochet the pattern, plus how many skeins you'll need. Also included is that specific yarn's "yarn weight." You'll find this information on the label of every skein of yarn you buy, and it ranges from #0 lace weight to #7 jumbo weight. If you can't find the specific yarn I use or you'd like to use something else, knowing the yarn weight will help you pick another yarn that will have the same gauge.

Standard Yarn Weight System

Categories of yarn, gauge ranges, and recommended needle and hook sizes

Yarn Weight Symbol & Category Names	0 LACE	1 SUPER FINE	2 FINE	3 LIGHT	4 MEDIUM	5 BULKY	6 SUPER BULKY	7 JUMBO
Type of Yarns in Category	Fingering, 10-Count Crochet Thread	Sock, Fingering, Baby	Sport, Baby	DK, Light Worsted	Worsted, Afghan, Aran	Chunky, Craft, Rug	Bulky, Roving	Jumbo, Roving
Knit Gauge Range in Stockinette Stitch to 4 inches*	33–40 sts**	27–32 sts	23–26 sts	21–24 st	16–20 sts	12–15 sts	7–11 sts	6 sts and fewer
Recommended Needle in Metric Size Range	1.5–2.25 mm	2.25–3.25 mm	3.25–3.75 mm	3.75–4.5 mm	4.5–5.5 mm	5.5–8 mm	8–12.75 mm	12.75 mm and larger
Recommended Needle in U.S. Size Range	000 to 1	1 to 3	3 to 5	5 to 7	7 to 9	9 to 11	11 to 17	17 and larger
Crochet Gauge Ranges in Single Crochet to 4 inches*	32–42 double crochets**	21–32 sts	16–20 sts	12–17 sts	11–14 sts	8–11 sts	7–9 sts	6 sts and fewer
Recommended Hook in Metric Size Range	Steel*** 1.6–1.4 mm Regular hook 2.25 mm	2.25–3.5 mm	3.5–4.5 mm	4.5–5.5 mm	5.5–6.5 mm	6.5–9 mm	9–15 mm	15 mm and larger
Recommended Hook in U.S. Size Range	Steel 6, 7, 8*** Regular hook B–1	B–1 to E–4	E–4 to 7	7 to I–9	I–9 to K–10½	K–10½ to M–13	M–13 to Q	Q and larger

* GUIDELINES ONLY: The above reflect the most commonly used gauges and needle or hook sizes for specific yarn categories.
** Lace weight yarns are usually knitted or crocheted on larger needles and hooks to create lacy, openwork patterns. Accordingly, a gauge range is difficult to determine. Always follow the gauge stated in your pattern.
*** Steel crochet hooks are sized differently from regular hooks—the higher the number, the smaller the hook, which is the reverse of regular hook sizing.

Source: Craft Yarn Council of America's **www.YarnStandards.com**

Notes on the Instructions

- When a number appears before the stitch name, such as 3 dc, work these stitches into the same stitch—for example, "3 dc into the next st."
- When only one stitch is to be worked into each of a number of stitches, it can be written like this: "1 sc in each of next 3 sts." When a number appears after a chain—for example, "ch 10"—this means work the number of chains indicated.
- The asterisks mark a specific set of instructions that are repeated—for example, "* 2 sc in next st, 1 dc in next st; rep from * across" means repeat the stitches from the asterisk to next given instruction.

- When instructions are given with parentheses, it can mean three things—for example, "(2 dc, ch 1, 2 dc) in the next st" means work 2 dc, ch 1, 2 dc all into the same stitch. It can also mean a set of stitches repeated a number of times—for example, "(sc in next st, 2 sc in next st) 6 times." Last, the number(s) given at the end of row or round in the parentheses denote(s) the number of stitches or spaces you should have on that row or round.
- Be sure to read the Special Stitch(es) and Pattern Note(s) sections before beginning a project. You'll find any new stitches and helpful hints there, and reading these notes will often clear up any questions about the project.

Abbreviations

beg	begin/begins/beginning
BLO	back loop only
BPdc	back post double crochet
BPsc	back post single crochet
ch(s)	chain(s)
ch-	refers to chain or space previously made
ch sp(s)	chain spaces(s)
cl(s)	cluster(s)
cm	centimeters
dc	double crochet
dc2tog	double crochet 2 stitches together
dc3tog	double crochet 3 stitches together
FLO	front loop only
FPdc	front post double crochet
FPsc	front post single crochet
FPtr	front post treble crochet
g	grams
hdc	half double crochet
hdc2tog	half double crochet 2 stitches together
in	inches
lp(s)	loop(s)
mm	millimeter
oz	ounces
rep(s)	repeat(s)
rnd(s)	round(s)
RS	right side
sc	single crochet
sc2tog	single crochet 2 stitches together
sk	skip
sl st(s)	slip stitch(es)
sp(s)	space(s)
st(s)	stitch(es)
tog	together
tr	treble
WS	wrong side
yd(s)	yards

How to Hold Your Hook

There are different ways that you can hold your hook, but I want to show you two of the most common. Try both, and use the one that feels most comfortable.

Knife Hold: Hold the hook in your hand like you would a knife. Your hand is over the hook, using your thumb and middle finger to control hook while the pointer finger is on top guiding the yarn.

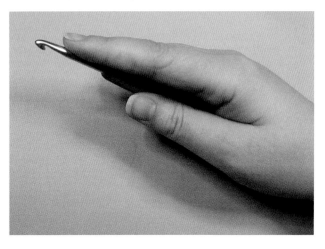

Pencil Hold: Hold the hook like you would a pencil. The hook is cradled in your hand and resting on your middle finger.

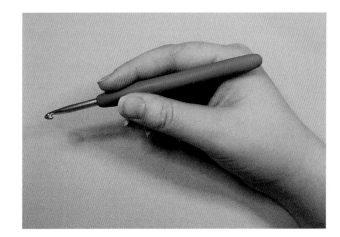

STITCH GUIDE

Slipknot
This adjustable knot will begin every crochet project.

1. Make a loop in the yarn.

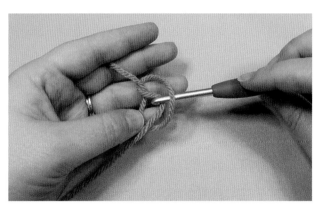

2. With crochet hook or finger, grab the yarn from the skein and pull through loop.

3. Pull tight on the yarn and adjust to create the first loop.

Chain (ch)

The chain provides the foundation for your stitches at the beginning of a pattern. It can also serve as a stitch within a pattern and can be used to create an open effect.

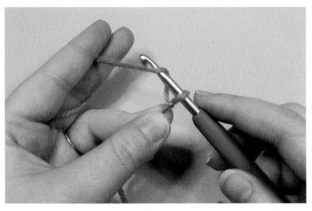

1. Insert hook through the slipknot and place the yarn over the hook by passing the hook in front of the yarn.

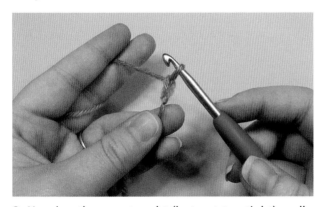

2. Keeping the yarn taught (but not too tight), pull the hook back through the loop with the yarn. Ch 1 is complete.

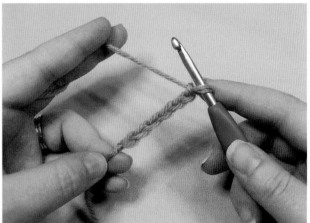

3. Repeat steps 1 and 2 to create multiple chains.

Single Crochet (sc)

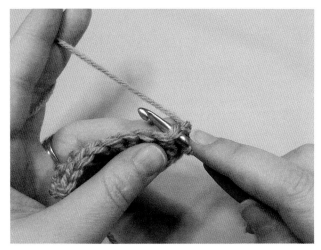

1. Insert hook from the front of the stitch to the back and yarn over.

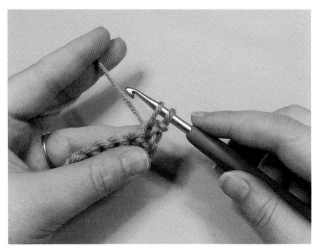

2. Pull the yarn back through the stitch: 2 loops on hook.

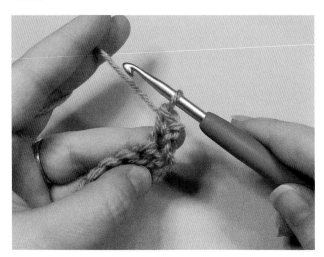

3. Yarn over and draw through both loops on the hook to complete.

Working into a Stitch

Unless specified otherwise, you will insert your hook under both loops to crochet any stitch.

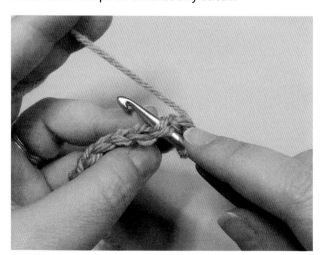

Working into Back Loop or Front Loop

At times you will be instructed to work in the front loop only (FLO) or the back loop only (BLO) of a stitch to create a texture within the pattern.

Insert hook to crochet into the front loop only (FLO) of a stitch.

Insert hook to crochet into the back loop only (BLO) of a stitch.

Slip Stitch (sl st)

The slip stitch is used to join one stitch to another or to join a stitch to another point. It can also be used within the pattern as a stitch without height.

1. Insert the hook from the front of the stitch to the back of stitch and yarn over.

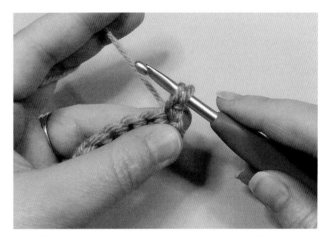

2. Pull the yarn back through the stitch: 2 loops on hook.

3. Continue to pull the loop through the first loop on the hook to finish.

Half Double Crochet (hdc)

1. Yarn over from back to front over hook.

3. Yarn over and pull yarn back through stitch: 3 loops on hook.

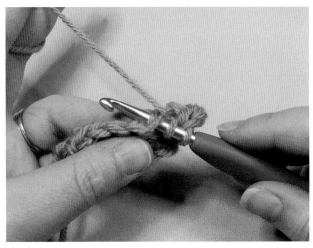

2. Insert hook from the front of the stitch to the back.

4. Yarn over and draw through all 3 loops on hook to complete.

Working in the Half Double Crochet "3rd Loop"

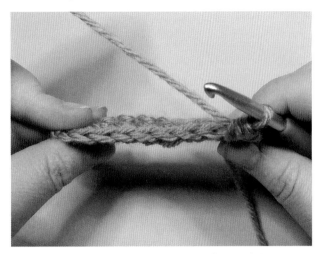

1. Locate the top loops you normally work into.

3. Work into the hdc 3rd loop as you would a regular stitch.

2. On the WS (or back side) of the hdc, you'll see a horizontal bar. This is the 3rd loop of the hdc.

Double Crochet (dc)

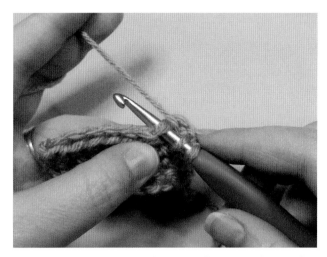

1. Yarn over and insert the hook from the front of the stitch to the back.

3. Yarn over and draw the yarn through the first 2 loops on the hook: 2 loops on hook.

2. Yarn over and pull the yarn back through the stitch: 3 loops on hook.

4. Yarn over and draw the yarn through the last 2 loops on hook to complete.

Treble Crochet (tr)

1. Yarn over 2 times.

2. Insert the hook from the front of the stitch to the back. Yarn over and pull the yarn back through the stitch: 4 loops on hook.

3. To complete: (Yarn over and draw the yarn through the first 2 loops on the hook) 3 times.

Single Crochet 2 Together (sc2tog)

A single crochet 2 together (also known as a decrease) will take two stitches and make them into one single crochet stitch.

1. Insert the hook from the front of the stitch to the back and yarn over. Pull the yarn back through the stitch: 2 loops on hook.

3. Yarn over and draw through all 3 loops on the hook to complete.

2. Leaving the loops on the hook, insert the hook front to back in the next stitch. Yarn over and pull back through stitch: 3 loops on hook.

Double Crochet 2 Together (dc2tog)

A double crochet 2 together will take 2 stitches and make them into one double crochet stitch.

1. Yarn over and insert the hook from the front of the stitch to the back. Yarn over and pull the yarn back through the stitch: 3 loops on hook.

3. Leaving the loops on the hook, yarn over and insert the hook from front to back into the next stitch. Yarn over and pull back through the stitch: 4 loops on hook.

2. Yarn over and draw the yarn through the first 2 loops on the hook: 2 loops on hook.

4. Yarn over and draw the yarn through the first 2 loops on the hook: 3 loops on hook.

5. Yarn over and draw the yarn through all 3 loops on hook to complete.

Double Crochet 3 Together (dc3tog)
A double crochet 3 together will take 3 stitches and make them into one double crochet stitch.

1. Yarn over and insert the hook from the front of the stitch to the back. Yarn over and pull the yarn back through the stitch: 3 loops on hook.

2. Yarn over and draw the yarn through the first 2 loops on the hook: 2 loops on hook.

3. Leaving the loops on the hook, yarn over and insert the hook from front to back into the next stitch. Yarn over and pull back through the stitch: 4 loops on hook (shown in photo). Yarn over and draw through first 2 loops on hook: 3 loops on hook.

4. Leaving the loops on the hook, yarn over and insert the hook from front to back into the next stitch. Yarn over and pull back through the stitch: 5 loops on hook.

5. Yarn over and draw the yarn through the first 2 loops on the hook: 4 loops on hook.

6. Yarn over and draw the yarn through all 4 loops on hook to complete.

169

Working on the Post of the Stitch

Each stitch has a post. When working a front post stitch or back post stitch, use the post instead of the top stitch. This is the DC post.

Front Post Double Crochet (FPdc)

1. Yarn over and insert the hook from the front to the back to the front around the post of the stitch.

2. Yarn over and pull the yarn back around the post: 3 loops on the hook.

3. Complete like a double crochet: Yarn over and draw the yarn through the first 2 loops on the hook: 2 loops on the hook. Yarn over and draw the yarn through the last 2 loops on the hook to complete.

Back Post Double Crochet (BPdc)

1. To work the back post double crochet, simply work from back to front to back around the post and complete steps 2 and 3 as for front post double crochet.

3. Complete like a double crochet: Yarn over and draw the yarn through the first 2 loops on the hook: 2 loops on the hook. Yarn over and draw the yarn through the last 2 loops on the hook to complete.

2. Yarn over and pull the yarn back around the post: 3 loops on the hook.

Front Post Treble Crochet (FPtr)

1. Yarn over twice, insert hook from front to back to the front around the post of the stitch.

2. Yarn over and pull the yarn back around the post.

3. (Yarn over and draw through 2 loops on hook) 3 times.

Reverse Single Crochet (rev sc)

Single crochet worked from left to right (right to left, if left-handed).

2. Yarn over, draw through all loops on hook.

1. Insert hook into next stitch to the right (left), under loop on hook, and draw up a loop.

Color Change
When changing colors, use this technique:

1. Complete your given stitch until the last pull-through.

3. Continue working with joined color.

2. Yarn over with the next color and pull through to finish the stitch and color change. Cut or drop the yarn from the original color.

ACKNOWLEDGMENTS

First, I must thank my family for their continued support—mainly my wonderful husband, Jason, who supports my yarn-y creativity! To my eagle-eyed pattern editors, Christina Romich and Vicky Heimbecker: I appreciate your many hours of edits and patience. Next, to my stitch assistants, Tabatha Widner and Vicky Heimbecker: thanks for all you've contributed! And I can't forget to thank my many testers . . . this has been an adventure, and I'm glad you joined me! I love how this book has come together and am grateful for all those who have been a part of the process.

Photography for this book was by Heather, with Heartstrings Photography, in her beautiful studio in Huntsville, Alabama. And lastly, many thanks to my cousin, Ciji, and her great family—Jason, Luke, and Tessa—for joining the fun and allowing your family to model.

VISUAL INDEX

Angel Wings
Garland   2

Ava Motif
Blanket   6

Monster Pillow   10

Baby Catchall
Tote   14

Stuffed Rattle
Toy   18

Snuggle Time
Sleepersack   22

Trendy Diaper Pail
Cover   26

Precious Hanging
Lanterns   30

Briar Wall
Hanging   34

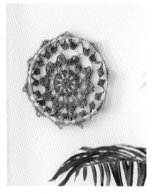

Blooming Wall
Hanging   38

Diamond
Curtains   42

Kolby Mandala
Rug   46

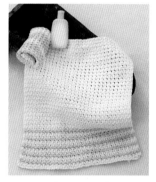

Bobble Pillow   112

Briggs Cable
Blanket   114

Hot-Air Balloon
Mobile   118

Daydream
Blanket   122

Ultimate Storage
Basket   126

Carter Basket   130

Bear Lovey   134

Handy Wipes
Case   138

Woodland
Loafers   142

Relaxing Footstool
(Pouf)   146

On-the-Go
Backpack   150

Curtain Tie   154